Ryder and Yates

Twentieth Century Architects

Engineering Research Station, Killingworth

Ryder and Yates

Twentieth Century Architects

Rutter Carroll

THE
TWENTIETH
CENTURY
SOCIETY

ENGLISH HERITAGE

RIBA Publishing

© Rutter Carroll, 2009

Published by RIBA Publishing, 15 Bonhill Street, London EC2P 2EA

ISBN 978 1 85946 266 9

Stock Code 67263

British Library Cataloguing in Publications Data
A catalogue record for this book is available from the British Library.

Publisher: Steven Cross
Commissioning Editor: Lucy Harbor
Project Editor: Susan George
Editor: Ian McDonald
Designed & typeset by Carnegie Book Production
Printed and bound by the Charlesworth Group, Wakefield

RIBA Publishing is part of RIBA Enterprises Ltd.
www.ribaenterprises.com

Front cover photo: Ryder House, Woolsington, 1969.
Back cover photo: Gordon Ryder and Peter Yates, c. 1971.

Foreword

I regard myself as extremely fortunate to have spent part of my career under the tutelage of three great architectural figures – Gordon Ryder, Peter Yates and Ted Nicklin.

Their passion and unswerving dedication to contemporary architecture – as a force for good in the world – infused every aspect of their lives. It was nothing less than a way of life and an inspiration to me.

We need to understand the past in order to face the future with confidence, and without them I would not have become the person I am and Ryder would not be the company it is now.

It is a privilege and a delight to be writing this foreword for the first book to recognise and chronicle what is, I believe, a highly significant body of work, a fitting testament to the value of Ryder and Yates.

I like to think that their spirit lives on in Ryder today.

By Peter Buchan, Chief Executive of Ryder

Acknowledgements

The sources of this book are many, as I have tried to show in the references, but in particular are the publications of the architectural press and the archives of Ryder, formerly Ryder and Yates.

I am indebted to Mary, the widow of Gordon Ryder, who willingly allowed access to all of Gordon's personal papers, and to the family of Peter Yates, his widow Gilly, and their children, Sally Ann, Libby, Adam and Jolyon, who have given so liberally of their time in assisting me.

I am grateful to Colum Giles and Elain Harwood of English Heritage, to Alan Powers of the Twentieth Century Society and to the Royal Institute of British Architects for offering me the opportunity of publishing this work.

To Peter Buchan of Ryder, former staff of Ryder and Yates, and the owners and occupiers of their buildings, I am indebted for their help and cooperation.

Finally, I should like to thank my wife Kathleen for her encouragement and constructive criticism in the preparation of this typescript.

Rutter Carroll, Gosforth, 2009

Opposite: St Paul's Cathedral, London, Peter Yates, 1940

"Without the Twentieth Century Society an entire chapter of Britain's recent history was to have been lost. It was alert when others slept. It is still crucial!"

Simon Jenkins, writer, historian, journalist

Love it or hate it, the architecture of the twentieth century has shaped our world: bold, controversial, and often experimental buildings that range from the playful Deco of seaside villas to the Brutalist concrete of London's Hayward Gallery.

Arguably the most vibrant, dynamic and expressive period of architecture in history, the twentieth century generated a huge range of styles. You don't have to love them all to believe that the best of these exciting buildings deserve to be protected, just like the masterpieces of the Victorian era, many likewise once thought to be eyesores. Buildings that form the fabric of our everyday life — office blocks, schools, flats, telephone boxes, department stores — are often poorly understood.

The campaign to protect the best of architecture and design in Britain from 1914 onwards is at the heart of the Twentieth Century Society. Our staff propose buildings for listing, advise on restoration and help to find new uses for buildings threatened with demolition. Tragedies like the recent demolition of modernist house Greenside, however, show how important it is to add your voice to the campaign.

Join the Twentieth Century Society, and not only will you help to protect these modern treasures, you will also gain an unrivalled insight into the groundbreaking architecture and design that helped to shape the century.

THE
TWENTIETH
CENTURY
SOCIETY

www.c20society.org.uk

Contents

Ryder and Yates office staff c. 1968

Introduction

I first became aware of the architecture of Ryder and Yates as a student of architecture in Newcastle in the early 1970s. Prior to attending university I had worked for the engineer Ove Arup and, consequently, my student research studies focused on Arup's role in the development of modern architecture in England through his association with Berthold Lubetkin and the Tecton practice. I met both Arup and Lubetkin on several occasions and they drew my attention to the work of Gordon Ryder and Peter Yates. John Allan has since confirmed that they were the only architects of that generation Lubetkin ever admired.[1]

As there was no comprehensive account of the work of Ryder and Yates, I embarked on a thesis to examine their architecture in detail. This journey led to the discovery of a diverse range of buildings of extraordinary maturity within the modernist canon. This was architecture of distinction, though not well known – perhaps due to its location in the North of England – but it clearly demonstrated the artistic and theoretical ideals of the Modern Movement, essentially carrying on from where Lubetkin's career had been cut short, but appropriate to the conditions of a later age.

Ryder and Yates demonstrated innovative thought, combined with an unshakable belief in the validity of their ideals that was at once responsive to its location and to the demands of its strongly regional client base. The result was an architecture that was regional, yet also national and even international in the scope of its ideas and in its calibre.

A few simple but strong principles and motifs guide Ryder and Yates's work from 1953 until Yates's death in 1982. Once formed, these principles changed little, and Ryder and Yates doggedly resisted the changing fashions of the 1960s and 1970s. They had a strong grounding in classical architecture. Peter Yates began a lecture to the Royal Institute of British Architects in November 1975 by quoting Alberti saying that a city should be 'for the convenience of its inhabitants and a surprise to its visitors'. 'We share a love of surprises,' he added.[2] He also acknowledged Palladio for his organisation of classical motifs, the Taj Mahal with its central volume surmounted by turrets and minarets, and Viollet-le-Duc's ideal cathedral with its towers. They admired classical architecture, yet the image-forming power of its geometry could prove 'a sepulchre', faced with the need for a building to change, or what Yates termed 'energy and growth'. Their best work contains both traits.

However, Ryder and Yates were not influenced by the contemporary design of their peers, having no major influences apart from their acknowledged mentors, Le Corbusier and Berthold Lubetkin. These influences, through the forceful personality of Gordon Ryder and the persuasiveness of Peter Yates, spread within their open-plan office.

While Lubetkin had never been in any doubt about his debt to Le Corbusier, he was not quick to acknowledge the fact; Yates by contrast would discuss Le Corbusier's work at great length with his staff. But then Yates was in the unusual position of having known Le Corbusier personally from his years in Paris and through working with his closest English correspondent, Clive Entwistle.

Like Le Corbusier, Yates used his art not only to inform his three-dimensional design but also to adorn his own work in the form of murals, 'murals that build walls or destroy them – an artificial horizon'. Yates described art as 'an assembly of forms', as first seen when, as a child in Venice, 'coming out of a dark alley I saw the sun sparkling across a plazza and was moved to tears'.[1] While this was common in the heroic period of the Modern Movement, it became increasingly rare in post-war England. Moreover, both Ryder and Yates had gone on to work for Lubetkin as part of a small team assembled to build the new town of Peterlee in County Durham. They were not alone in pursuing a modernist agenda, but this personal connection to two great masters was unique, and gave their borrowings a real authenticity.

It is said that Lubetkin did not draw, but encouraged the skill in others. This was certainly true of Gordon Ryder. Ryder admired Lubetkin but had not got on with him, unlike Peter Yates who had the benefit of having known him earlier in London. A common misconception about the workings of the practice was to see Ryder as the businessman and Yates as the designer. This was based perhaps on the public personas of the gregarious Ryder and the introspective Yates; however, their personalities and working methods were more complex. Ryder's was the principal hand in the layout of a scheme with Yates taking responsibility for realising much of a building's form, as well as its decorative features. Yates spoke in his lecture of Ryder having 'a balance of talents, and without him none of this would have happened'.

It has been suggested, too, that the practice would have gained far more recognition and commissions had it moved to London. But this was never considered. Both partners loved the North East of England and felt it the ideal place to bring up their large families; the proximity of the North Sea meant that Ryder could indulge his passion for sailing, while Yates could paint the Northumbrian countryside that he loved.

The world that emerged from the early 1950s saw Ryder and Yates eager to move beyond the limitations brought by post-war economic and political turmoil. The first buildings showed a remarkable maturity despite the lack of real projects handled by either of them. While they had both worked on the design and master planning of Peterlee, none of their work was realised. Their architecture developed through the experience of building and the repeated use of generic themes and philosophies. It was possible to read elements in these of the International Style, but there was a wide range of materials and many quirks in the planning and elevational treatments.

Such modern buildings appeared revolutionary to the planning committees of the small northern local authorities in which they were built, and this earned Ryder and Yates the reputation of being rogue architects. Yates suggested that the time had come to compromise. Ryder refused, believing that their architectural principles were precious and should never change. As a result, the practice had to wait until 1960 before securing its first major commission, a car showroom and workshop for a local Ford dealer. Tales of triumph over adversity bind each generation of architects as they tackle their first major projects. For Ryder and Yates, the problems they experienced with the planners during the design and construction of the Tonner House were vindicated by the presentation of a Civic Trust Award.

This refusal to compromise paid off in the 1960s with major commissions from Newcastle Corporation, Northern Gas and Northumberland County Council. Northern Gas stands out as a particularly supportive client, notably in its preference for local architects over those based in London. In the 1960s, Ryder and Yates's office expanded rapidly to meet this workload, and eventually required a new building. The new office was open-plan and specifically designed to limit the staff numbers to 40. This meant that everyone, partners, architects and engineers, could see at first hand what was being produced, and also that Ryder and Yates themselves could maintain close control over all the work. The practice earned five major architectural awards, including two RIBA awards.

Although almost no reference has been made in this book to individual members of staff, that is not to diminish their role in the execution of the partnership's buildings. While the authorship of the buildings by the two lead partners is indisputable, Ryder and Yates have a special significance as one of the country's first truly multi-disciplinary practices, where architects and structural, mechanical and electrical engineers worked together from the start in realising a design. The partnership reached maturity when in 1963 it was formally joined by the Polish engineer Leszek Kubik, confirming a multi-disciplinary approach that gave a deeper understanding of the processes of building. Later, in 1966, a mechanical engineer, Jack Humphrey, and another architect, Ted Nicklin, joined and also became partners. Compare this with the Building Design Partnership which was founded as a multi-disciplinary practice by George Grenfell Baines in April 1961, and Arup Associates founded by Sir Ove Arup, Philip Dowson, Ronald Hobbs and Derek Sugden in 1963, and we see that Ryder and Yates were in the vanguard of this new way of working; they also came to involve dedicated contractors in the evolution of their buildings from an early stage.[4] And by 1975 Yates could not imagine another way of working.

The economic decline of the 1970s coincided with a reaction against modernism. Architects and planners, as creators of the physical environment, were labelled as the perpetrators of the problems that were besetting the inner cities. Comprehensive redevelopment, system building and new towns became bywords in an era of urban unrest and social deprivation. A younger generation of architects turned to vernacular styles, particularly for housing. This influence was felt in Ryder and Yates's office, but led to a compromise rather than the total abandonment of modernist ideals and practices.

This is well seen in their housing at Albany, Washington, County Durham, where the planning reflects the experience of Peterlee but is expressed architecturally in pitched roofs – albeit stylised ones – and traditional load-bearing brickwork. Gordon Ryder was never satisfied with the scheme, and in some ways it reflected more deep-rooted changes to the office. Peter Yates was in poor health, Leszek Kubik left for academia, and new staff brought different ideas into the practice.

This book is an attempt to reveal the principles of design particular to the architecture of Ryder and Yates. To this end it is structured by building type, looking at their housing, exhibition work, buildings for commerce and industry, and social and welfare buildings. Within each type, the buildings are considered chronologically. It is only by bringing together the many projects of Ryder and Yates that the generic themes of their work can be recorded and analysed.

There are key elements that are worth emphasising. The design of each building type, even with the varying briefs and locations, shared a common approach. Despite the apparent simplicity of the early houses and exhibition work, they established a basic orthodoxy for everything that followed. All their buildings were site-specific, responding to the particular character of the area in which they were to be built, taking into account the micro-climate, topography, vegetation and any existing features or structures. The materials used were indigenous to the location, whether bricks, stone or timber, and could be used in a vernacular fashion.

Ryder and Yates were culturally aware of the northern location in which they practised, and this had an effect on the way they approached their design. No attempt has been made to include every building by the practice; rather the aim is to provide an overview of the wide variety of work completed during 30 years of practice from 1953 to 1982. The exclusion of any particular building is no reflection upon its quality or interest.

The book has concentrated on Ryder and Yates's built work, and not their many unrealised projects and competition entries. One ambitious proposal by them, in 1968, was to bridge the River Tyne between Newcastle and Gateshead via the creation of a structural deck that could serve a new City of Tyneside council, the river being controlled through a series of locks. Realising in the 1960s that the river would never service large ships again, they looked to regenerate the derelict quayside areas north and south of the river which were being ignored by their respective councils, with a scheme that was influenced by their work on the central complex at Peterlee. Predictably it came to nothing, though the principle of joint government was acknowledged with the creation of the Tyne and Wear County Council in 1974. The quayside areas have been extensively developed in recent years, notably with the Crown Courts, Sage Music Centre, Millennium Bridge and Baltic Art Gallery.

Ryder and Yates accumulated a number of awards and honours for their buildings, and Gordon Ryder was awarded an OBE. The practice has continued as the Ryder Nicklin Partnership, latterly simply as Ryder, which operates throughout the UK while acknowledging the important foundations and heritage left by the founding partners.

This book has been commissioned as part of a shared initiative between the Royal Institute of British Architects, English Heritage and the Twentieth Century Society, to chronicle the work of British post-war architects. The Ryder and Yates practice has been identified by these organisations as the most important post-war regional architectural practice. I am grateful to Matthew Thompson of RIBA, Colum Giles and Elain Harwood of English Heritage and Alan Powers of the Twentieth Century Society for offering the opportunity to publish this work. Elain Harwood, in turn, would like to extend thanks to Jolyon Yates and Peter Willis for their help in the project.

Rutter Carroll, Gosforth, 2009

Notes

1   John Allan, the biographer of Berthold Lubetkin, to the author, May 1993.
2   Peter Yates, 'Architects' approach to Architecture', *Architects' Journal*, vol. 162, no. 46, 12 November 1975, p993.
3   Ibid.
4   'Ryder and Yates and Partners', *RIBA Journal*, vol. 83, no. 1, January 1976, p28.

Corbu, a painting by Le Corbusier and Peter Yates, date unknown

CHAPTER ONE:
Early Years

Ryder ...

John Gordon Ryder was born on 5 December 1919 in Thornaby-on-Tees, outside Middlesbrough, the son of a bookmaker.

His formal education was cut short in 1930 as a result of a childhood accident, a serious leg break while rock climbing, which later excluded him from war service. Thereafter, Ryder developed practical skills, which was to be integral to the way in which he was to approach design. He had a passion for technology, which he was able to explore in detail with the building of model steam engines from scratch, something that he continued to enjoy throughout his life. In 1936 this passion was directed into architecture and he entered articles with a Middlesbrough firm of architects, William Edwin Haslock.

In the 1920s and 1930s the North East was the most depressed part of England, if not of Britain, and there was little opportunity for new building. Peter Yates later claimed that there was no modern architecture in the north when they set up their practice,[1] but this was not quite so, for there were modern houses by local architects Cackett, Burns Dick and McKellar in Newcastle, and by Leslie Martin and Sadie Speight at Rock, Northumberland, and BBC studios by Wells Coates, Secretary of the MARS (Modern Architecture Research) Group and a member of the Congrès Internationale d'Architecture Moderne.

Such groups addressed not only design but also the way that life should be lived, embracing an ethical outlook as well as formal values, and also making close studies of history and industrialisation as part of the process of making architecture and urban plans. By the late 1930s these ideas had permeated the School of Architecture at King's College, in Newcastle but constitutionally part of Durham University. The origins of the School are uncertain, but it was formally established around 1920 under Reginald Cordingley and expanded following the appointment of Wilfred Edwards as head in 1933, with Thomas Sharp running courses in town planning from 1936.

In 1940 Ryder entered King's College as an RIBA probationer to read architecture under Edwards. For a time – until they were unceremoniously evicted in 1942 – he shared rooms with another architecture student, who would become a lifelong friend, Peter 'Brutus' Smithson, also from the North East. Smithson went on to serve in the armed forces, but Ryder completed his course, qualifying in 1944. He then undertook postgraduate study at Newcastle in town planning under Sharp, and in 1945 was

Gordon Ryder, c.1940

Peter Yates, self portrait, c.1940

appointed a studio demonstrator at the School of Architecture. Among his first-year students was Alison Gill, later to become Smithson's wife. Ryder left his teaching post only in 1948, to join Berthold Lubetkin at Peterlee.

... and Yates

Whereas Ryder was born, educated and worked entirely in the North East, Peter Yates's background was more exotic. He was born in Wanstead, Essex, in 1920, and after leaving school he worked as a commercial artist in Fleet Street, covering international exhibitions in Paris and Glasgow. He turned to architecture in 1938, studying at the Regent Street Polytechnic under Sir Hubert Bennett, Robin Day and Peter Moro. Moro, a committed modernist and Corbusian acolyte, had arrived in London before the war as a refugee from Nazi Germany. He came with an introduction and promises of work from Walter Gropius, who had already emigrated to London from Germany. When Gropius offered no work, Moro was fortunate to find a position in the office of Tecton, the practice set up around a Russian émigré, Berthold Lubetkin. Something of Moro's sense of form, pattern and colour can be seen in Yates's work.

From 1941 Yates worked briefly as a fireman, and painted the incendiary attacks on London while on watch at St Paul's Cathedral. He joined the army in 1942, studying radio engineering at Queen's College, Belfast, in Malvern and at the Science Museum in Kensington, before embarking with the Advance Field Unit of the Allied Expeditionary Force to Normandy and setting up a transmitting station at the Palace of Versailles. Yates put his skills as an artist into views of Paris. As a member of the liberating army in Paris, Yates took time to seek out Le Corbusier's atelier and, finding him dishevelled, offered food and supplies. There began a friendship that would last until Le Corbusier's death in 1965.

Peter Yates wrote of this meeting with Le Corbusier in a memoir in 1967.

> Rue Nungeser et Coli,
> Porte Molitor
> 1944
>
> Le Corbusier apologised, 'See how we are under the Germans' – his dark brown leather jacket looked completely worn out. His shoes had thick wooden soles like sabots with uppers of straw basketwork, and lined with cat fur.
>
> We sat at the white marble table in the dining room which links, like the web of an H, Le Corbusier's small living room to his large studio.
>
> 'Can we see your paintings?' I said. He came out of his chair like an eagle and his eyes shone. 'You like painting? You are a painter yourself?' And round that marvellous room he went, full of excitement, pouring armfuls of drawings onto the low tables: drawings of stones and women and flowers and fish and fir cones. There were thick portfolios labelled 'drawings L.C.' down through the years and neat brown paper parcels protecting mounted drawings and labelled 'Bulls', 'Women', 'Ubus'.[2] He was back with a vast roll of canvasses that he unrolled, hurling each across the floor, one after another: wrestlers and lovers; stones, bones; giant women with purple fruits and rainbow scarves; great shells perforated by the sea; chestnut leaves unfurling out of sticky buds; fishes and clouds and rocks and ropes.
>
> He showed how he worked, on writing paper thin enough to trace one drawing from another: retaining some parts, altering others. Using coloured chalk then brushed over by water to unify the colour and bring it to the edges of its form. In all these drawings there was a wildness and accidental life not evident in the monumental and more finely coloured hard edge oils.
>
> 'Would you like one? Choose which you like,' he said, shovelling 50 or so onto the table. I found three nude giantesses, one bright pink, one grey and one white with bright blue hair, all holding hands and sitting on a rock. I fell in love with them.
>
> 'You like them?' he asked, wrote my name in the corner 'amicalement' and signed it Le Corbusier.[3]

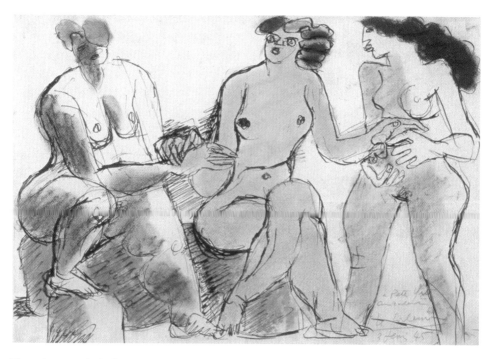

Three giantesses by Le Corbusier dedicated to Peter Yates, Paris 1945

George Braque in his Paris studio 1945, Peter Yates, c.1977

As well as Le Corbusier, Yates met a wide circle of artists and intellectuals including Gertrude Stein, Alice Toklas, André L'Hote, Sylvia Beach, Edward Pignon, Jaime Sabartes, Juliette Greco, Leon Gischia and André François.

During his time in Paris, Yates saw a plaque outside the house of the painter Georges Braque; he knocked and inquired if the great man did painting lessons – fortunately he did.[4]

After demobilisation in January 1946, Peter Yates worked with Ove Arup as an architectural draughtsman, mainly on his entry with Clive Entwistle and Jørgen Varming for the Crystal Palace competition announced the year before. (The Crystal Palace competition was announced in March 1945 for a cultural and sports centre to replace Paxton's masterpiece, destroyed by fire in November 1936. It was a wildly optimistic project for the years of austerity after the war, commissioned by aged trustees with no funds to realise it, and in 1952 the park was passed to the London County Council.)

Entwistle himself had courted Le Corbusier's friendship and provided another link to the great man. But more importantly, it was while working for Arup that Yates first met Berthold Lubetkin, who was working with Arup on a number of revived Tecton projects. The Crystal Palace design owed much to Yates's draughtsmanship skills, but although its glass pyramid was widely admired as a modern variant on the old building and for its technical brilliance, it was unplaced. The first prize went to a classically inspired design, but this too was never built.

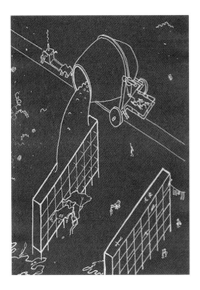

Christmas card by Peter Yates for Ove Arup

Yates later worked for Entwistle in his Paris office, Unité d'Informations Visuelles, on a range of industrial designs that included electric pencils, pneumatic tents, record changers and audio equipment, in addition to work in architecture and exhibition design. Yates remained in touch with Arup, for whom he designed Christmas cards, and he continued to develop his painting, which while clearly evolved out of the European modernist tradition is infused with a gentler English palette and sense of humanity.

By 1948 Berthold Lubetkin was appointed architect planner at Peterlee and he asked Yates to join his development team for the design of the new town.

Notes

1   Peter Yates, 'Architects' approach to Architecture', in *Architects' Journal*, vol. 162, no. 46, 12 November 1975, p993.
2   Le Corbusier completed a number of paintings with this in the title, typically, 'Etude pour sculpture Ubu – "Panurge"'.
3   Extract from a memoir of Le Corbusier by Peter Yates, 1967. Courtesy of Yates papers.
4   Cyril Winskill, Journal newspaper, Dec 15 2006

CHAPTER TWO:
Berthold Lubetkin and Peterlee

'We learnt everything from Lubetkin,' Gordon Ryder is quoted as saying.[1]
'We learnt from Lubetkin that nothing is fixed', said Peter Yates.[2]

For Ryder and Yates aged, respectively, 29 and 28 in 1948, Peterlee was their most formative period, while Lubetkin, then at the age of 47, already had a legacy of learning and experience from across Europe that had flowered triumphantly in London in the 1930s. From the beginning, Lubetkin was aware that art and architecture had a deep-rooted social purpose, and he found that this view was consolidated by the writings of Karl Marx.

As a student, Lubetkin had had three quests: to understand philosophy in order to give his work direction, to look at European traditions in art, and finally to study modern building methods.[3] Russia's weak economy and the backward state of its building industry led Lubetkin to leave in 1922 for Berlin, where he witnessed the latest building techniques and absorbed the theories of the new German school of art history.

His goal was to find an architecture based on radical but rational philosophy that employed progressive techniques founded on classical principles. He began to compose his buildings in a classical sense, recognising that all composition involves a deliberate choice, a relation of parts and internal organisation reflecting in outline the concept of order.

By 1925 Lubetkin was in Paris, which offered him an opportunity to test those classical principles in exchanges with other artists. His architecture matured rapidly, as seen in the block of flats, 25 Avenue de Versailles, that he designed in association with J. Ginsberg, and which was built in 1928–31.[4] His only building outside England, these flats were the first realisation of Lubetkin's architectural ambitions.

However, a profound belief in socialist principles, and a perception of the role of art and architecture in the reconstruction of society following the Great War, set Lubetkin apart from his architectural contemporaries, and on moving to England in 1931 he looked to move from a theoretical position to realising these ideals in built form. The buildings he created for animals at London Zoo in 1932–4 provided an intellectual basis that he developed in subsequent projects. On a more modest scale, Ryder and Yates were to use exhibition design as a means of working out the intellectual base that they later brought to their architecture.

Another parallel between the work of Ryder and Yates and that of Lubetkin lies in

Opposite: St Paul's Cathedral west door, Peter Yates, c.1938

the latter's Highpoint I of 1935, particularly in the design of its ground-floor spaces. Lubetkin admired the way in which artists such as Georges Braque could produce structured designs using an interplay of form. In Highpoint I, this interplay was held in check by the overall frame, against which forms were juxtaposed – curved against rectilinear, sharp against smooth, patterned against plain.

His Highpoint II, begun in 1936, was a very different statement, its design intended as a reminder of classical values and the importance of order. This building provided still more ingredients for Ryder and Yates's later style, for its rectangular frame was juxtaposed by a curved cantilevered entrance canopy and ramp, and topped by a penthouse flat, added by Lubetkin for himself, with a parabolic-arched concrete roof. These elements appear frequently in Ryder and Yates's work.

Lubetkin's belief that new architecture should be an agent for human betterment was realised in the projects that he designed for Finsbury Borough Council in London, particularly its health centre, completed late in 1938. This work attempted to maintain the guiding principles of the past in a new fusion with those of the present, using modern construction methods.

Of all the modern buildings erected in the 1930s, Finsbury Health Centre was arguably the best dress rehearsal for the democratic architecture based firmly in new technology that came to the fore after the war. It adopted a lightweight construction

The Bonny Pit Lad, Peter Yates, c.1952

for the wings – containing the consultation and treatment rooms – in recognition that these parts of the building should be able to change.

The post-war years should have been a triumphant time for Lubetkin, as his ideals of modern architecture in the service of a fairer society were vindicated, and in 1948 the post of architect planner at Peterlee seemed to offer the perfect platform for him to realise his ideas on a grand scale. However, continuing planning issues and conflict between the key players would ultimately result in his departure.

The idea of a new town on the Durham coalfield began in 1943 when the Ministry of Health asked local authorities to assess their post-war housing needs, and to prepare a housing programme for immediate implementation after the war. Easington Rural District Council, in the east of the county, sought a longer-term strategy, and proposed building houses and amenities away from declining pithead villages on five new sites. Then their engineer and surveyor, C. W. Clarke, suggested centralising development in a single location near Old Shotton. It was not the only post-war new town to be created to supply a shortage of amenities for an existing industrial base, but the idea of creating a central focus for isolated rural communities was unique. Miners were to move from their huddled terraced housing around the pitheads into a new commercial, recreational and administrative centre. Light industry was to be developed to provide alternative employment, as well as forming part of a long-term strategy as the pits were worked out.

Clarke set out his ideas in a pamphlet, *Farewell Squalor*, in 1946, which extended even to a name for the new settlement. Peter Lee was a local miner who had discovered temperance and risen to become the general secretary of the Durham Miners' Association in 1930.[5]

Lubetkin rejected the artificiality of the new town concept and its garden city associations when first approached to design one by Lewis Silkin. But he became persuaded by the idea of a progressive miners' community that would be properly urban.

The chairperson of the Peterlee Development Corporation was Monica Felton, a socialist intellectual and governor of the London School of Economics who had served on the committee appointed by Reith to set up new towns and who promised employment opportunities for women. Her aspiration was to compensate the miners for what she saw as their organised betrayal in the General Strike of 1926.[6]

Some years later, Ryder and Yates wrote:

1947 AD

The war is over. Peterlee is to be the symbol of the Brave New World, the complete contemporary town, as big as Durham City. For the miners, Peterlee took the name of a great miners' leader and it was to take compelling account of a social problem.

This vivid idea was due to C. W. Clarke, Surveyor, later milk roundsman and now in the service of Jesus Christ.

His proposal was to develop at high density one town, which would form a centre to the circle of collieries. These settlements, as Monica Felton said, are neither town nor village. They are mining camps – but camps built with a terrifying permanence. The site chosen for the new town was superb: a natural marvel, comparable with Durham and the major sites of Europe. An unspoiled, little known 'lost world' in a shallow saucer completely containing its own landscape.[7]

On being appointed, Lubetkin wrote to Felton, 'I have an infallible conviction that the proper concern of architecture is more than self display. It is a thesis, a declaration, a statement of the social aims of the age. Its compelling geometrical regularities affirm man's hope to understand, to explain and control his surroundings. By thus asserting itself against subjectivity and equivocation, it discloses a universal purposeful order and clarity in what often appears to be a mental wilderness.'[8]

Such was Lubetkin's reputation that when he advertised for staff to form a planning team at Peterlee he received several hundred applications (though accounts of the actual number vary hugely, with up to 3,000 being suggested) – this at a time when many authorities were struggling to secure and retain staff. Gordon Ryder was, it seems, the only applicant from the North East, and his qualifications in town planning made him a strong candidate. He was duly appointed, along with David Goldhill, Frank and Mary Tindall, Florian Vischer and Peter Yates. This formed the nucleus of Lubetkin's development team.

Lubetkin's plan was utopian, more in the mode of Le Corbusier's plan of 1942 for Saint-Dié than in the British garden-city tradition adopted by the other new towns. He saw the site for Peterlee as a basin, with the whole town set within it, allowing the exclusion of all views of the surrounding coal mines. Lubetkin was committed to the idea of a densely populated town, with a compact grouping of tall or large buildings around its centre. The classically inspired arrangement of three slab blocks, one at the apex and two at the base, was referred to by Yates as being 'like the jaws of a chuck', pointing towards a notional centre with lower public buildings and shops grouped in a variety of geometric forms. These public buildings were bisected by a main road cutting right through the town, with bridges across the ravines of Castle Dene to the south, with their 'primeval forest snaking up and narrowing at the centre'.[9]

Lubetkin's team at Peterlee, in the gardens of Shotton Hall, c.1948 (Peter Yates second left, Gordon Ryder middle)

The Denes at Peterlee, Peter Yates, c.1952

The site chosen was one of outstanding natural beauty on the surface, but below lay five workable coal seams, which were to create almost insurmountable problems. The master plan had to be based around the plan for the systematic extraction of the coal and the consequent subsidence problems for the land above.[10]

In advance of Lubetkin's appointment, the Ministry of Town and Country Planning had made important concessions to the National Coal Board (NCB) to ensure that there was no opposition to the new town designation. They were an inadequate basis upon which to prepare a master plan.

A small area was released by the NCB in the corner of the town at Thorntree Gill for housing, but it insisted on retaining its mining options elsewhere. As a result, no site could be agreed for the more substantial buildings required in the town centre, or for schools and public buildings. Meanwhile the Ministry insisted on a master plan based on the assumption that the extraction problem did not exist. Thus began the planning problems that were to beset Peterlee. As the NCB adopted a hard-line approach, and the Ministry became confused by its early promises, the original intentions for the new town changed. The plans were revised in order to allow the building of the outer housing estates without any agreement on the centre.[11]

Although prepared to alter other details, Lubetkin was adamant about retaining the three high-rise blocks designed to give the centre such a strong form and identity, to which later development would not have to conform, but which required the coal seams below to be sterilised. The NCB would not accept this. Lubetkin would not accept a new policy of low density and slow growth, which would effectively downgrade the initial programme of 500 houses per year to 100 and achieve only half of the target population. He and Felton's successor, Lord Beveridge, reached a stalemate. Mary Tindall, one of the last surviving members of the Peterlee team, remembers a disastrous row. With no agreement in prospect, the whole design team was sacked when Lubetkin allowed his tenure to lapse in 1950.[12]

Lubetkin retired to the farm in Gloucestershire that he had acquired during the war, purportedly to take up pig breeding. He did, however, also form a new practice, Skinner, Bailey and Lubetkin, which completed three housing schemes for Finsbury Borough Council and took on three more in Bethnal Green. Yates returned to Paris, and Ryder went back to Newcastle to set up his own small practice. There is nothing officially recorded, but Ryder later suggested that Lubetkin had offered him not only the job of Peterlee's architect/planner, but also the sale of his penthouse in Highpoint II, though not necessarily at the same time.

Although nothing had been built in their three years at Peterlee, the experience of working with Lubetkin enriched Ryder and Yates's architectural vocabulary and reinforced their modernist values. Peter Yates executed many of the exquisitely rendered presentation drawings for the new town, which showed the influence of his work with Clive Entwistle. Gordon Ryder worked with him on a project for 100 houses at Thorntree Gill, a series of cubic dwelling units with lower links to form terraces.[13]

Their responsibilities included preparing the elevations and design models which, because of the topography, were to symbolise beads down the hillside.

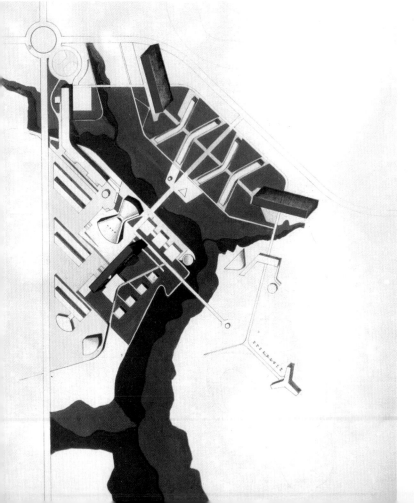

Peterlee Master Plan, c. 1950

Wheatley Colliery, Durham, Peter Yates, c.1957

This architectural imagery would reappear in later work by Ryder and Yates, first in their competition entry for Carlisle Civic Centre, then at Killingworth and, in particular, in their housing development at North Kenton in Newcastle.

Notes

1   Gordon Ryder, interview with author, November 1984, Newcastle.
2   Peter Yates, 'Architects' approach to architecture', *Architects' Journal*, vol. 167, no. 46, 12 November 1975, p993.
3   Peter Coe and Michael Reading, *Lubetkin and Tecton – Architecture and Social Commitment*, Arts Council of Great Britain, 1981.
4   25 Avenue de Versailles, Paris, 16. Arr. 1928–31, J. Ginsberg and B. Lubetkin, reviewed in *Architectural Review*, vol. 72, 1932, pp133–8.
5   C. W. Clarke, *Farewell Squalor – A New Town and Proposals for the Redevelopment of Easington Rural District*, report to Easington Rural District Council, December 1946.
6   Monica Felton, 'Peterlee New Town', *Architect and Building News*, vol. 194, no. 4169, November 1948, pp410–12.
7   Ryder and Yates, 'The Poetry of Peterlee', *Northern Architect*, no. 6, p112, September 1962.
8   Berthold Lubetkin, letter to Monica Felton, Peterlee, 13 July 1947, quoted in Coe and Reading, op. cit., p17.
9   Gordon Ryder's notes for his 'Architects' approach to architecture' lecture, part quoted in *Architects' Journal*, 12 November 1975, p993.
10   *Peterlee, Analysis of Planning Problems*, Report of the architect/planner, 16 April 1950. Prepared by Gordon Ryder, whose copy, no. 48, was kindly given to the author by Jack Lynn.
11   Ibid.
12   Coe and Reading, op. cit., pp181–6; and John Allan *Berthold Lubetkin, Architecture and the Tradition of Progress*, RIBA, London, 1992, pp281–5.
13   Letter from Gordon Ryder to Emma Read, a student at Newcastle University, 1 February 1994; courtesy Ryder papers.

CHAPTER THREE:
House Style

The new houses do not rely on the imitation of well-known features. Their effect is achieved by more simple means – by simple shapes, which accentuate the native richness of cedar wood, cherry red brick, quarried stone and white paint. The general shape of the exterior of the two houses has been determined by the open planning of the interior, together with central heating, features not yet common in this country.[1]

Gordon Ryder

The permanent buildings from Ryder and Yates's first years in practice were almost all individual private houses. Commissions were sporadic and unpredictable, and limited by the licensing of all building materials until November 1954. Consequently, more time was spent on competition work which, while financially unrewarding, provided an opportunity to develop new ideas. The most interesting of these competitions was that held by the City of London for new housing at Golden Lane.

Ryder's simple formal arrangement of four blocks, inspired by Peterlee, was linked by broad access ways or 'promenades' at every third level, and developed with another ex-Newcastle student, Jack Lynn. Alison and Peter Smithson's entry used a similar access arrangement, which they called 'decks', linking asymmetrical blocks of different lengths.

Neither scheme won, that honour going to Geoffry Powell with a mix of high and low blocks arranged in courtyards. However, Lynn was to develop the idea of promenades or deck-access housing further in a student project with Ivor Smith and then in a real scheme for Sheffield City Council, Park Hill. Peter Smithson later claimed:

The word deck appears for the first time anywhere (outside a boat) on our Golden Lane competition drawings of 1952, and the report gives an explanation of the attitudes that lie behind its adoption.

Gordon Ryder (the dispatches lost him somewhere) and Jack Lynn submitted a scheme for the same competition. It had access balconies but was not specially developed as social spaces as far as we can recall, and stylistically the design was related to the flat blocks of Tecton, for Gordon

Opposite: Interior of Damerell House, Scotby 1956

Ryder worked with Lubetkin at Peterlee and was the inheritor of his design method.[2]

The first project executed by Gordon Ryder's fledgling office was a new clubhouse for the Tynemouth Sailing Club, of which he was an enthusiastic member, in 1952–3. Here he met three of his most important early clients, Derek Damerell, J. Kenneth Stanger and James Liddell, who shared his love of sailing.

In 1953, Ryder began work on an exhibition stand for the Carlisle Plaster Company at Olympia. During a visit to London he met Yates, quite accidentally, on an underground station. It transpired that Yates had been unwell and did not wish to return to Paris, so he agreed to join Ryder in Newcastle on the basis of sharing work and profits – 'we paid ourselves £5 a week'.[3]

From the outset the office had a strong commitment to modernism and a desire to see it built. But planning committees, shocked by their proposals, delayed or rejected their early applications, and occasionally even suggested that their client find another architect. 'The time had come to compromise,' Yates recalled, when reminiscing to the RIBA in 1975. Yet Ryder retorted, 'Never! We'll do what we believe in and be known for it. And one day someone will come along and ask us to design something big.'[4] At the time, Yates did not believe him, but Ryder proved to be right.

Further commissions for houses followed, and a second premium in the Carlisle Civic Centre competition helped to raise the profile of the practice and make it respectable. The turning point came when they designed a house in Tynemouth for Jack Liddell and his family. The journalist Anne Glidewell labelled it 'a stunner' in a special women's week feature in the *Daily Express*, which caught the eye of the Northern District Manager of Martins Bank.

The design of 14 private houses across the North, of which 12 were built, demonstrated recurring themes in plan, form and use of materials which characterised Ryder and Yates's work. All owe something to Le Corbusier, but there is a greater diversity. The houses were specific to each client and site, without an obvious generic approach; the organisation of the plan played the dominant role in the design.

Generally with narrow linear plans, sequentially organised, the houses emphasised their major spaces with secondary areas included in linked pods. The carefully designed elevations, with key elements such as the entrance marked by a dramatic sculptural incident, seemed to derive from Lubetkin's work. The plans also used devices clearly derived from Le Corbusier such as the division of spaces by columns or staircases, and they explored the relationship between internal and external spaces. All featured a dominant fireplace. Columns were also used structurally, to permit facades to be entirely glazed.

Innovation was clear in the inventive means of construction and the mix of new and traditional materials. Roofs were always flat but were animated by roof lights, canopies, chimneys and water tanks, often boldly articulated. Historical references were made in the use of materials or a detail, or in murals by Yates.

Design for a sailing club, c.1952

The first house designed by Ryder after Peterlee was that for Dr Walker in Woolsington Park, Newcastle; it was designed with Jack Lynn and completed in 1952. As key workers, doctors enjoyed a special dispensation in securing building licences and they made up a high proportion of Ryder and Yates's early clients. Unlike all the designs that followed, the planning for the Walker house was based on the use of three intersecting squares set at 45 degrees. Circulation within the house was reduced to an efficient minimum, rejecting the English convention of dividing up spaces off a central corridor, in favour of a more relaxed and open-plan lifestyle. The importance of a dominant living space had become a common theme in Lubetkin's work that can arguably be traced to the dacha, the informal Russian out-of-town house.

In the Walker house, the intersecting squares imposed a strict geometry on the plan. They produced odd corners that were used to good effect, and the shape gave the advantage of creating an extremely long sitting room (16 m) with a fully glazed wall giving access to the garden. Similarly, the all-glass wall to the front of the principal bedroom opened out onto a balcony, while the magenta-painted rear wall had a single, square, centrally placed window that became, in Yates's words, 'an eyeglass on the world'.[5]

The Walker House, Newcastle upon Tyne, 1952

The freestanding fireplace, with its trapezoidal brick flue repeating the geometry of the house, stood centrally in the living room. It was clearly a functionalist statement and one which would be repeated in all the other houses. The central heating boiler, meanwhile, was positioned in the hallway with the staircase wrapped around both it and the cylindrical white flue, which in turn extended up through the open stairwell to the roof. This was an early expression of the practice's balance between functionalism and theatricality.

The house was constructed of traditional materials, load-bearing brickwork and timber windows with a felt-covered mono-pitched roof. Ryder suggested a copper roof covering but the client declined this in an effort to keep costs down, something he regretted in later years.

Ryder's next project was an unexecuted scheme of 1952–3 for two houses in Beadnell on the Northumberland coast, a favourite weekend retreat and holiday destination for North East families. The three-storeyed houses were designed for Audrey Stanger, the wife of a Newcastle surgeon, and her sister Jean. They met with great resistance from local residents, and also from planners – several of whom had second homes in the area.

The houses were to be modernist statements of exposed reinforced concrete frames, infilled with panels of stone and timber; they also had roof gardens. They were a strict interpretation of Le Corbusier's 'five points', with free facades, free plans, flat roofs, strip windows and pilotis.

William McKeag, a Newcastle solicitor and councillor who owned a house in Beadnell, led the objections to Ryder's designs, and eventually a public inquiry ensured that they would never be realised. A perspective[6] had been commissioned from Peter Yates, who was in London at the time, to appease the planners, but it had the opposite effect. By exaggerating the height, the drawing convinced the council that the houses were too tall, unsympathetic and should be rejected. The houses were reported in the local paper as 'stark monstrosities, vulgar, ostentatious buildings erupting in the sky dominating and dwarfing all the surrounding place'.[7]

Although they were never built, the houses had an important place in Ryder and Yates's work. When T. Dan Smith, the Newcastle council leader, invited Eric Lyons to design a new housing scheme at North Kenton he declined but recommended Ryder and Yates on the strength of a review of the Beadnell beach houses he had read in *Architectural Design*.[8]

The design also influenced the painter Victor Pasmore during one of his many visits to Ryder and Yates's office when he was preparing house type elevations for Peterlee.[9] Pasmore was appointed in 1955 as the development corporation's consultant advisor in the design and layout of housing for Peterlee's south-west area, to bring back something of the visionary quality lost with Lubetkin's departure. He put forward a case to have Ryder and Yates appointed as consultants to the Peterlee development team, but the general manager, Vivian Williams, who had earlier ordered the destruction of all Lubetkin's drawings and reports, would have none of it and actively discouraged Pasmore from visiting their office.

Ryder and Yates's first house in formal partnership was built in 1954 for Derek Damerell at Scotby in Cumbria. Again it brought them into conflict with the local authority. Damerell had shared an office with Ryder in Newcastle and both were active members of Tynemouth Sailing Club, so when he was appointed as a director

Stanger Beach Houses at Beadnell, drawn by Peter Yates, 1953

The Damerell House from the South East

Plan of the Damerell House, Scotby

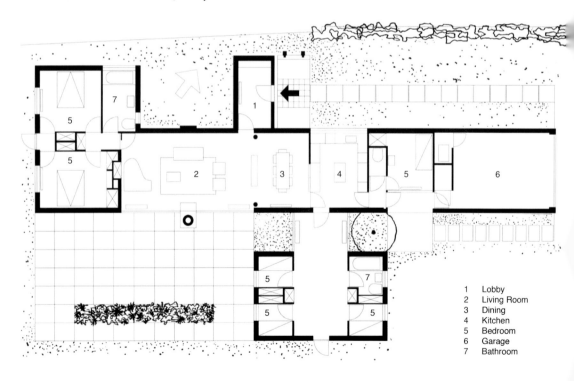

1   Lobby
2   Living Room
3   Dining
4   Kitchen
5   Bedroom
6   Garage
7   Bathroom

of Carlisle Plaster and Boards he duly commissioned a new house in the area. He also commissioned Ryder and Yates to design the first of a series of exhibition stands for the company.

The Damerell house, called Harlequin, was built in the paddock and orchard of a Georgian house. It was a more mature and sophisticated design than the projects for Walker and Stanger. A single-storey load-bearing brick construction with a flat roof, it adopted a sequential plan that began with the garage, and led through the kitchen, dining room and living room to bedrooms at the more secluded end. This linear plan was an early example of Ryder's favourite planning technique, which would be subsequently applied to a variety of building types. A ceremonial route alongside the dwelling had a protective curved canopy, another device that would be repeated in future houses, and heralded the main entry – placed centrally in a surprisingly classical manner. The children had their own wing, with bedrooms and a bathroom opening off a playroom, attached to the kitchen by a glazed link.

The entire south wall of the main living space, opening to the garden, was glass, with the chimney and the greater part of the fireplace set outside it and supporting the roof structure. Storey-height twin parabolic roof lights, finished internally in gypsum plaster to show off the client's wares, presented clerestory sunlight to the living area both morning and evening, and transformed the flat roof.

Two white columns demarcated the lounge from the dining area, where the only natural light came through a circular roof light set in a black enamelled ceiling over the table. Natural lighting to the bathroom area was via a glazed wall consisting of two layers of ply glass enclosing a sheet of translucent silk, chosen because, in the architects' words, it 'admits light, ensures privacy and retains warmth'.[10] The kitchen was comprehensively fitted with purpose-made cabinets containing the latest electrical appliances, with a double-glazed servery to the dining area. Parabolic canopies extended over the two entrances to indicate their location and offer protection.

Peter Yates's formidable artistic skills were used to good effect, not only for murals in both the entrance hall and kitchen, but in the evident contribution to the three-dimensional form, making what was the first acknowledged Ryder and Yates design. Drawings and early sketches of the house showed, in his painterly way, geometric mounds and angular trees set in front of the elevations – a foretaste of what he would later term 'earth sculpture'.

The house has been extensively remodelled, and is almost unrecognisable from the original design. All the principal roof lights and canopies have been removed to permit the installation of a traditional pitched roof over the house and children's wing, which had already been extended. The fate of Yates's murals is unknown.

Also completed in 1954 was a small, single-storey farmhouse at Walton, near Brampton in Cumbria. The Stevens' farmhouse at Hill House Farm was less conventional than many of Ryder and Yates's larger and more immediately striking designs. The brief was simple. The house had to be constructed for no more than £1,400 and should include a large dining area for the farm workers in addition to the normal

Hill House Farm, Brampton, 1954

Layout of Hill House Farm

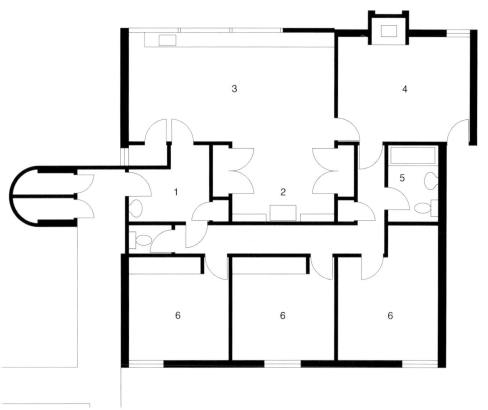

1 Lobby
2 Kitchen
3 Dining
4 Living
5 Bathroo
6 Bedroo

The Tonner House, Hayton. View from the main road

private areas for the family. This compares with the £8,350 it cost for J. T. Laing to build Harlequin in the same year.

The setting was magnificent, as befitted a hill farmhouse, and the resulting little modernist building dominated the area. Built of brick with contrasting panels of white render and timber, it enclosed a rectilinear plan with bedrooms at the rear, and living rooms to the southern front. The entrance, like that of the Damerell House, was sideways to the main elevation, this time with a curved entry porch that was flat-roofed and featured an oversized concrete waterspout.

The southern, garden, elevation was carefully composed of differing materials to produce an effect of light and dark. The sculptural form of the externally expressed fireplace and flue were echoed, in reverse, in the rainwater hopper head and pipe, each containing a U form cut into the face as a symbol of tension. This feature would recur in some form in most of their subsequent work, particularly at their own office in Killingworth. Internally, as expected of a working farmhouse, the fixtures and fittings were simple, with 'All-day' sliding windows able to take advantage of the spectacular views across the valley.

The design for a small house, Friar's Garth, in Hayton, Cumbria, for J. F. Tonner, a lecturer at the Rutherford College of Technology, became a *cause célèbre* when it was presented to the local planners. Ryder and Yates proposed a single-storey, flat-roofed, two-bedroomed house of traditional construction, with walls of concrete block and a curved stone wall to the main living area. The steeply sloping site elevated the building and necessitated an external concrete stair, giving it greater impact than would normally be expected of a single-storey dwelling.

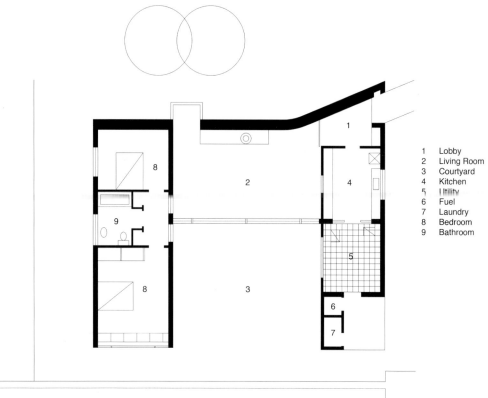

Layout of the Tonner House

1	Lobby
2	Living Room
3	Courtyard
4	Kitchen
5	Utility
6	Fuel
7	Laundry
8	Bedroom
9	Bathroom

Friar's Garth was designed to harmonise with the village of Hayton, and in particular the adjacent parish church, in its use of materials. The house also incorporated a series of historic references. A Gothic oriel, albeit rectangular and of steel but set against curved stone walls, echoed Lubetkin's use of classical statuary in the curved entrance to Highpoint II. This was the first use of a curve in Ryder and Yates's planning; prompted by that of the adjoining main road, it was to subsequently feature in all their major works. The main entrance, in its way as ceremonial as that of the Damerell House, was the first use of a partial lobby wall, usually curved and which served as a lung or 'spatial valve' between the hall and the rooms it served. This was another Lubetkin reference, taken from the weekend bungalow he had designed for himself at Whipsnade.[11]

The chimney, of concrete but patterned in the manner of Sir John Vanbrugh's Seaton Delaval Hall a few miles north of Newcastle, completed the historical metaphors. The use of such references as symbols would become an important component of Ryder and Yates's design idiom, indebted to Lubetkin's Highpoint II with its caryatids, but taken much further, and more closely tied to local materials and landmarks.

An oversized cubic fireplace dominated the living room where two white columns supported the roof over fully glazed walls overlooking the garden. The internal corridor serving the bedrooms was lit by a domed roof light which, together with a circular water tank, repeated motifs from the earlier houses to create a lively roofscape.

The design was initially rejected by the rural district council and county planning authority, but was allowed on appeal, when the Ministry of Housing and Local Government overruled the recommendation of its inspector, and it was finally completed in 1956 at a cost of £4,000. The house later received a Civic Trust award, the irony being that the chairman of the planning committee, Lt Col. T. Fetherstonhaugh, had declared that the house would only be built over his dead body. Now he had the ignominy of making the presentation. He excused himself to the local paper, explaining that 'at the time, I think we were slightly amazed that a house of that type was to be built in a village like Hayton, but all architecture is modern at some time. I think there was a certain amount of criticism of St Paul's Cathedral and Regent Street.'[12]

The original form of the house is still intact, although the windows have been replaced and the flat roof upgraded.

Tonner's new house inspired one of his colleagues, Charles Oakley, to commission a design from Ryder and Yates in the adjoining village of Hayton Head. This was for an extension, built in 1957, to a traditional stone and slate Cumbrian cottage, and it gave the architects a chance to work with an existing building.

The old house was self-contained and introverted, but their two-storey extension was clearly open and extrovert. Rather than attempt to replicate the original vernacular design, Ryder and Yates made a complete contrast by adding a living room in glass, with a timber-clad bedroom cantilevered over it. The spatial quality of the glazing not

Oakley House. View from the front garden

only emphasised the beauty of the old Cumberland stone, but also brought it into sharp contrast with the sandstone of a new gable.

This rubble wall was of triangular section and carried a ribbon of glazing between the floors, making the bedroom appear to float over the living area. It was also extended out to form a backdrop and shelter to the south-facing terrace. The familiar cubic fireplace and cylindrical flue, almost out of scale with the small living space, were contained internally with a receding wall and clerestory ribbon of glass running behind them. The historical references were subtle here, reserved for facing materials of cedar and stone, and in the traditional Cumbrian stone window surrounds. The roof was a parabolic arch, but asymmetrical, and was exposed internally in the bedroom.

Ryder and Yates wrote of the house:

> Lyrically set between pine forest and meadowland, an old cottage of beautiful stone, flecked with orange lichen. The problem was to build a sympathetic yet valid addition.
>
> Complete contrast was achieved by adding a glass living room with a single storey of grey cedar poised above it.
>
> The stone wall of triangular section carries a knife-edge of glass at its apex, giving a very light floating effect to the structure. It aids the spatial relationship of living room and garden and provides a sun-warmed sheltered corner in which to sit. The client has very pleasantly demon-strated al fresco meals here, with snow upon the ground![13]

The glass wall and stone gable to the ground-floor living area have since been removed and replaced with a fenestration of timber boarding, standard casement windows and door.

A more complex house was that designed for Dr Thomas Saint in 1956, creating family accommodation and a separate surgery on a site within a suburban housing estate in Longbenton, Newcastle. As high-rise flats and three-storey maisonettes overlooked the location, Ryder produced a single-aspect design – a favourite device of his – set at one side of the site, looking into a walled garden. Only on the first floor was an alternative aspect offered, from the secondary spaces of children's bedrooms and bathrooms.

The flat-roofed rectilinear house and its associated surgery and garage blocks were simple in form but achieved a modern character from the way the materials were used in their fenestration. The quintessential element of the Modern Movement was plain white walls, best formed from concrete but normally constructed of brick or block walls that were then cement rendered. In Saint House, concrete was used extensively but imaginatively in various forms of concrete brick, patterned, pre-cast concrete block and cast-in-situ concrete slabs. White timber boarding and in-situ concrete canopies with waterspouts – by now familiar Ryder and Yates motifs – appeared on the entrances to both house and surgery.

The Saint House and surgery, Newcastle. View from the south

The two-storey house had a linear plan of kitchen, dining room, hall and living room. This last room had a glass garden wall and a cubist fireplace, albeit one to a conventional scale and built into the end wall. The main entry was defined by paving at the mid-point of the dwelling, and was as ceremonial as that at the earlier Damerell House. Again there was a partial lobby linking the entrance hall with the rooms it served. A spiral staircase of steel, with rubber coverings to the treads, was enclosed in a concrete drum adjacent to the entrance, and its form extended into the lounge. The single aspect and sequential planning of the house meant that any natural lighting to the stair could only be via a circular roof light over the drum, which was used here to good effect.

The house, just one element in a tripartite composition, was set at right angles to the principal site access to give priority to the public surgery block and double garage, which were related to the road. The surgery, curiously, had no aspect either to the garden or to the main road, but was lit solely from clerestory windows running the length of the building to both front and back, and by roof lights over the ancillary spaces. This block has been demolished, but the house, now renamed 'Ryder House', has not been entirely compromised. New owners have resolved to refurbish the house according to the original design.

The builder James Liddell was a major supporter of the young practice, commissioning housing schemes in Tynemouth, Whitley Bay, Bournemouth and Torquay.

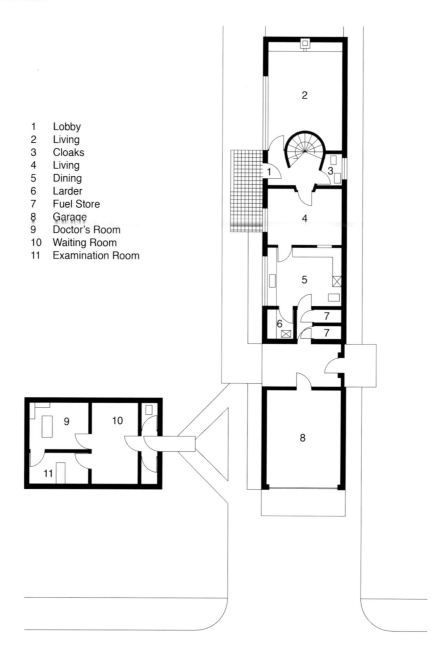

1   Lobby
2   Living
3   Cloaks
4   Living
5   Dining
6   Larder
7   Fuel Store
8   Garage
9   Doctor's Room
10 Waiting Room
11 Examination Room

Layout of the Saint House and surgery

He commissioned a house at Tynemouth for himself in 1958 which, because of its restricted site and eclectic details, was made the focus of a major feature on modern houses in the *Daily Express*.

You have to go far to find The House Where the Rainbow Ends. I have found it. It has colour. Space. Light. And warmth. And it glimmers – for a house like this couldn't just stand – by the sea at Number One, Grand Parade, Tynemouth.

It was a grey and misty day when I first saw it, but the brightly painted front door, set like a jewel among squares of coloured glass, blazed a welcome. The Liddells, who love the sea, could afford to let their architect have a free hand.[14]

Unlike their other domestic commissions, the three-storey, single-aspect town house for Liddell was designed for a tight urban site on the sea front. It differed from the earlier houses in that the ground floor was constructed from reinforced concrete and included a lattice screen to the street, which was inset with glass blocks, while the first and second floors were built in brick with ribbon windows.

Interior of the Liddell House, Tynemouth

The ingredients resemble those used by Ernö Goldfinger at Willow Road in London, but were pared down and more elemental, rather resembling a diminutive unit from Le Corbusier's Unité d'Habitation at Marseilles, completed in 1951. Part of the ground floor was given over to a service access to the adjoining property, while the remainder formed an entrance hall to the house. This was of particular interest for its extraordinary modelled plaster ceiling, which, together with a highly polished black and white chequered floor and mirror-faced doors, drew the eye to a mural by Peter Yates on the quarter landing. As Jack Liddell explained to the *Daily Express*, 'all we wanted of our entrance hall ... was something that would really startle our guests'.

An oversized parabolic arched fireplace dominated the first-floor living area, faced in patterned tiles set within a curved projecting base containing planting troughs. The gable wall behind the exposed flue was faced in mosaic, with 14 small marble brackets cantilevering out to display the client's collection of decorative teapots. The small kitchen was unremarkable, except for a Yates mural depicting food, which was complemented by another mural on the top landing of Brunelleschi's Dome in Florence. The historical referencing continued at roof level in the form of a Vanbrugh-style chimney similar to that at the Tonner House at Scotby.

Sadly, this remarkable house has been comprehensively remodelled, both inside and out. The feature ceilings, fireplace and display wall have gone, together with the murals. Externally the fenestration of the upper floors has been restyled, with the introduction of new windows in a different pattern and size from the original.

Ryder and Yates made a reputation as rogue modern architects with the public inquiry into the Stanger beach houses, and a house outside Morpeth, in Northumberland, brought them again into conflict with the planning authorities. The client was Alice Mamourian, from a wealthy Northumbrian land-owning family, who had lived in London for many years with her surgeon husband. On his death, and in her 71st year, she returned to Newcastle, where she sought the advice of Professor W. B. Edwards at the university on a suitable architect who could design a house for her on the family estate. Shirley Hewitt described the subsequent commission for readers of the *Sunday Sun*:

> Her instruction to 39-year-old architect Gordon Ryder and his partner
> Peter Yates was for an 'atomic cot, something concrete and modern'.
>
> 'I have always said that I would rather have one big room than be walled up
> in compartments – I can't be doing with it,' she told me.
>
> The white wood strip panelled entrance hall has no pretensions, yet is
> attractive. Like all the rooms of this house, it is meant to be used and lived
> in, so it is fitted with a washbasin without attempt at disguise. Explains
> Gordon Ryder: 'It is essential, though, to have a beautifully designed
> washbasin, so it looks like a piece of sculpture rather than a piece of
> sanitary equipment.'

South elevation of the Mamourian House clearly showing the alternating solid and void relationship between the floors

What a pity though that, because of its isolation, more people cannot see it. Maybe if it had been somewhere in town it may have gained many more converts for the cause of good modern building.[15]

The site was close to the old manor house, Stanton Hall, a 14th-century watchtower of a type common in the Border regions, to which had been added an 18th-century banqueting hall. The landscape had been formed into terraces, with a lower kitchen garden flanked by high brick walls and stone gateways. As the manor house became derelict, the high walls had collapsed and, together with the fallen gateways, provided a level plateau for building a new house. The historical element here was that the rear and end walls of the new house were to be built of the 18th-century bricks from the kitchen garden, and although the design would be uncompromisingly modern, there would be a clear link between old and new.

The simple rectilinear form had a single aspect and flat roof, and contained the obligatory glass wall between living room and garden, with the entrance set in a visually detached white timber box. Again the cubic fireplace with its cylindrical flue dominated the living space, but this time a square window was centrally placed in the end wall behind it. A simple open timber staircase demarcated the living room from the dining area in the open plan ground floor, while the separate kitchen kept circulation to a minimum.

The full glazing on the ground floor was transposed to slits on the first floor, set in vertical white timber boarding – the architects' logic was that you could have too much of a good thing, even when there was a spectacular view. The whole interior of the house was white, with a piranha pine stair, contrasting with black speckled linoleum

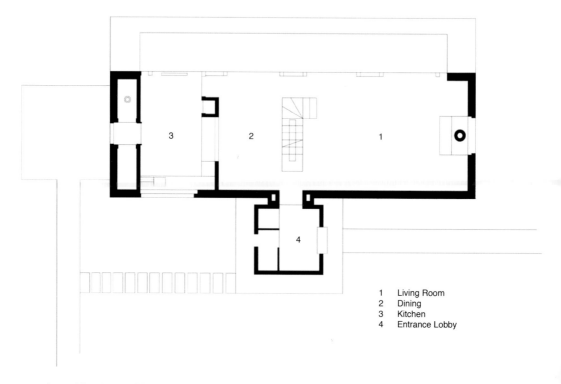

1 Living Room
2 Dining
3 Kitchen
4 Entrance Lobby

Ground floor layout of the Mamourian House

forming highly polished floors. A feature derived from Le Corbusier's villas was the use of sanitary fittings as items of sculpture.

As a result of the large projects now flowing into the office, the Mamourian house at Stanton, completed in 1959, was the last of the practice's one-off domestic designs, save for Gordon Ryder's houses for himself. The Mamourian house is in good order and largely unchanged, except for the replacement of the white vertical timber cladding with horizontal cedar boarding.

The design for the first Ryder family home, Trees, built at Woolsington and completed in 1967, was a combination of the Damerell and Saint houses in that it was planned as a progression of spaces, but with a children's wing integrated into the main volume. The main ceremonial entry to the house was similarly midway down the dwelling and again showed the use of a 'spatial valve' to link the entrance hall with the rooms it served. The entrance area also had a wall-mounted Grecian horse head, perhaps as a homage to Lubetkin. The general arrangement of the plan within the rectilinear 'shoebox' form provided for family and guest accommodation with an area for entertaining.

The Ryder House, "Trees", Woolsington. Garden elevation to the south

A separate area for the Ryders' four children related to the garden from individual study bedrooms and a sitting room, giving them total independence. A two-storey living area and first-floor rooms provided parent and guest accommodation, and the main bedroom had its own enclosed roof garden. The two-level living area, complete with Peter Yates mural, was contained within one volume, as at Le Corbusier's Unité d'Habitation, with a ceiling formed of two parabolic sections, one concave and the other convex.

It was envisaged to use the higher balcony informally and to retain the main floor, which related to the entrance, for reception and entertaining. The gable wall to this duplex was entirely glazed, giving extensive views across fields and parkland. Although a steel frame supported the parabolic ceiling over the living area, the structure generally was traditional load-bearing brickwork with selected external areas of Formica-faced ply panelling.

House and Garden magazine reported:

> Mr Ryder is engagingly unconventional in summing up the design of the house: 'As far as building techniques are concerned,' he says, 'the house, with minor exceptions, could have been built 50 years ago. Only the aesthetic is different – both visually and in terms of family needs. I think the house succeeds in providing an environment adequate for the whole family. The flexible plan allows parents and children to live together with what seems a minimum of friction and maximum enjoyment. Perhaps even more to the point, my wife agrees.'[16]

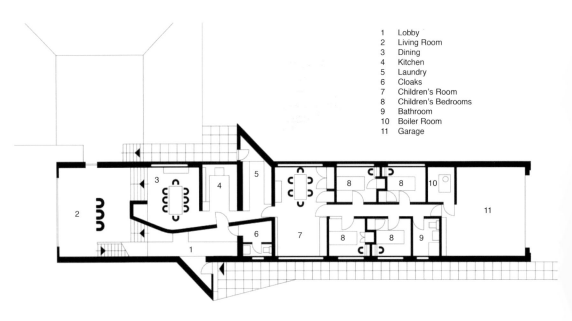

1	Lobby
2	Living Room
3	Dining
4	Kitchen
5	Laundry
6	Cloaks
7	Children's Room
8	Children's Bedrooms
9	Bathroom
10	Boiler Room
11	Garage

Ground floor plan of "Trees"

Or as the *Daily Mail* later recorded:

> When you walk into Gordon Ryder's house it would not be altogether surprising to find an engineering production line in full swing.

From the outside it is difficult to imagine anything less like a house or more like a factory. Mr Ryder does not mind the comparison.

He said: 'Most houses on this scale are designed to display the wealth of the people inside. What I've tried to achieve is a very private functional family house.'

He regards mass private housing by the big spec builders as generally good value for money. 'The designs can be reproduced ad infinitum and have been got down to a really fine art,' he said. But there could be improvements, including greater consultation between architects and potential buyers or council tenants on people's own design ideas and needs. He says, 'It is a tragedy that people are not consulted more.'

Mr Ryder suspects, however, that the conservative core of the British is against too radical change.

He observes a little acidly: 'Most British design is not exciting, but I do not think people want it to be. Builders who have ventured into the field of good design have usually burned their fingers.'[17]

The house remains as built, the only changes being replacement windows of a similar pattern and a new entrance door.

Completed in 1980 in Riding Mill, Northumberland, ten miles to the west of Newcastle, Triangles was a small house for the Ryder family and a more compact design than the grander project in Woolsington. It was designed to accommodate Gordon, his wife Mary, and guests, the children having now grown up and moved out. Inevitably, on completion the children moved back in!

The two-storeyed house followed the footprint of the original house on the site, Grey Manor. It was sequentially planned, with all rooms on both floors having a single south-facing aspect with views across the upper Tyne valley. The elegant, minimalist design was unusual in that it presented a blank flat-topped two-storey wall of stone northwards to the entrance road, and a sloping glazed wall to the south and garden terrace, resulting in an asymmetric section.

This was not quite the modernist solution Ryder had originally sought, but was a compromise with the local planning officer who had wanted a traditional design based on a Northumbrian farmhouse of stone and slate. After much dialogue and several abortive designs, the planner got stone and slate on the building, but not quite in the manner he had hoped.

The organisation of the plan was deceptively simple, with living and dining rooms, kitchen and garage arranged end-to-end in an extruded rectangle that deploys familiar devices. The entrance from the north is through a cubic pavilion – visually detached

The second Ryder House, "Triangles", at Riding Mill

Ground floor plan of "Triangles"

1   Entrance
2   Cloaks
3   Living Room
4   Dining
5   Kitchen
6   Garage
7   Workshop

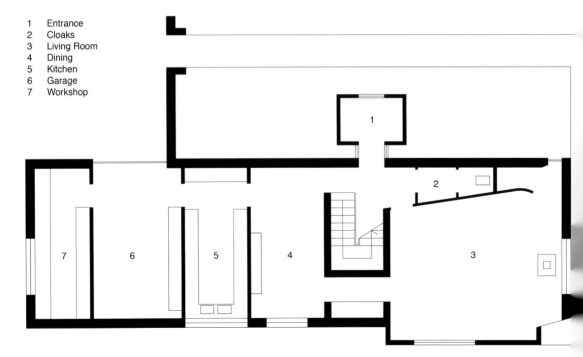

like that to the Mamourian house – while the central staircase is constructed in folded steel plate rather than timber.

Circulation is kept to a bare minimum and the obligatory detached fireplace, now a steel off-the-shelf model, is set in front of the gable window. A cloakroom to the entrance area allowed the introduction of a curved wall into the living area, and also screened a glazed storage area. On the north side of the first floor a narrow corridor, lit by a single circular window, centrally placed, linked bedrooms and bathrooms. The house remains as built.

Notes

1   Gordon Ryder, *Evening Chronicle*, 12 August 1954, p6.
2   Peter Smithson, *Architects' Journal*, vol. 144, no. 26, December 1966, p1590.
3   Peter Yates, 'Architect's approach to architecture', *Architects' Journal*, vol. 162, no. 46, 12 November 1975, p993.
4   Ibid.
5   See Peter Yates, 'Approach to Architecture', *RIBA Journal*, vol. 83, no. 1, January 1976, pp18–28.
6   This perspective was presented by Ryder to his friend E. Maxwell Fry on his 80th birthday.
7   *Evening Chronicle*, 1 September 1953, p4.
8   Gordon Ryder papers.
9   Garry Philipson, *Farewell Squalor, Aycliffe and Peterlee New Towns 1946–1988*, Aycliffe and Peterlee Development Corporation, 1988, p101.
10 Ryder and Yates, *Northern Architect*, no. 9, March 1963, p197.
11 John Allan, *Berthold Lubetkin*, London, RIBA, 1992, pp182–4.
12 *Cumberland News*, 18 January 1960.
13 Ryder and Yates, *Northern Architect*, op. cit., p197.
14 Anne Glidewell, *Daily Express*, 10 April 1958.
15 Shirley Hewitt, 'The Ultra-Modern House in the Heart of the Country', *Sunday Sun*, 30 August 1959.
16 Nicholas Drew, *House and Garden*, vol. 27, no. 1 (266), February 1972, pp46–9.
17 Roger Scott, *Daily Mail*, 1 April 1976.

CHAPTER FOUR:
Multi-occupancy Living

In 1954 the builder James Liddell commissioned a speculative scheme for tall flats on a site at Whitley Bay, on the coast outside Newcastle. The site formed part of the only major undeveloped area of land outside the green belt, and commanded a view of the Northumberland coastline. Nearby was St Mary's Island with its lighthouse, white against the blue sea and bays of golden sands. To the south lay the village of Cullercoats, famous for its smugglers' cave, lifeboat station and fishermen's cottages. Further along the coast was the Tynemouth headland, where the ruins of the priory, castle and haven dominated the skyline. To the north was Brier Dene, with its picturesque meandering watercourse and golf course, where Ryder and Yates designed two speculative houses in Brierdene Crescent. To the west, open farmland extended as far as Wellfield and the tower of Earsdon church, but elsewhere, a mass of undistinguished 20th-century development sprawled along the coastline.

Ryder and Yates proposed four 11-storey towers in a large green open space that was to be sheltered by mounding the earth sculpturally, and developed as a communal park. Yates conjured the words 'earth sculpture' to define his landscaping techniques of mounding earth in an obviously artificial manner supported by concrete. Beacon House, the first of the four blocks, was a first attempt at a development of a scale in sympathy with the magnificence of the natural environment nearby.

Ryder and Yates knew of Lubetkin's desire to build high in the master planning at Peterlee and, in 1954, Peter Yates had created a mural for Skinner, Bailey and Lubetkin's Y-shaped Bevin Court, one of their highly tactile blocks of social housing built in London for Finsbury MB. The Whitley Bay development was a first opportunity for Ryder and Yates to show what they could do in the realm of high-rise housing so popular with modernists.

Beacon House contained 44 luxury flats overlooking the sea on 11 floors, 'then referred to as a skyscraper', as Ryder later told a student.[1] It had the distinction of being the first multi-storey residential building in the North East of England. It showed a knowledge of sophisticated high-rise building techniques in reinforced concrete by using the plate floor system of construction, with external walls of cavity brickwork incorporating expanded polyurethane insulation.

The facing materials included white mosaic, with blue brindle brick set in panels below the pre-cast concrete windows to the front and rear elevations. The roofscape was

Opposite: The wall that says Lulu, Peter Yates, c.1976

Beacon House flats, Whitley Bay, Northumberland

animated by a circular enclosure for the building's water storage tanks. The entrance featured a perforated drum, and internally the walls of the communal areas were lined in Formica-faced timber panels, suitably endorsed with artwork by Peter Yates. The drum-shaped entrance and artwork correlate directly with Bevin Court. The complex was completed with garage courts, parking areas and considerable soft landscaping. However, Beacon House was the only one of the four towers originally proposed that was built; the rest of the site was used for a traditional low-rise housing development.[2]

The introduction of new windows and an incongruous skin of patterned brickwork to the gable wall have since altered it, although its essential form survives.

Social housing

Ryder and Yates looked for an opportunity to develop the ideas that they had initiated in their three months working on Thorntree Gill at Peterlee in their own social housing project. The chance came in 1962 with a major project at North Kenton for Newcastle City Council, and a smaller pilot scheme at St Cuthbert's Green, Fenham, started on site in 1963.

When Newcastle Council was selecting an architect for its proposed 'high profile' housing scheme at North Kenton, the last major open site within the city boundary, it first approached the Surrey-based architect Eric Lyons, a specialist in high-density housing for both the public and private sectors. This followed council leader T. Dan Smith's avowed intention to recruit the best-known architects, both nationally and internationally, for his redevelopment plans for Newcastle. Lyons declined the opportunity, but agreed to assist in the appointment of a local practice. He was familiar with the work of Ryder and Yates, and from a shortlist of names, supported by visits to their new clinics at Fawdon and Fenham, recommended them to the council. Ru Williams was the design architect in charge of the schemes, succeeded by Ted Nicklin.

Four of the eight house types used at North Kenton, including a specially developed and innovative courtyard type, were tested in a pilot scheme of 22 dwellings at St Cuthbert's Green, where local residents had successfully opposed the building of a 15-storey tower in 1960/61. Both St Cuthbert's Green and Kenton were to be designed around complete pedestrian and vehicular segregation. This was achieved at Fenham by extending the existing culs-de-sac at each end of St Cuthbert's Road to provide access

North Kenton estate, Newcastle

St Cuthbert's Green, Fenham

to the garages and hard standing, thereby leaving the remainder of the site vehicle free.

The housing was then grouped around an enclosed triangular precinct to create a village green. The development consisted of four terraces around a central court, with the western block stepped on plan into the court, reducing it to a triangle. This block included one-storey sections containing kitchen-diners, and two-storey elements with the living rooms and bedrooms.

The northern block, which fronted one of the access roads, contained seven three-storey terraced houses with integral garages. All the housing had flat roofs, but only this block exploited them with roof terraces, which were highlighted by a mono-pitched roof over the access door. A terrace of four houses, two storeys high with a single-storey kitchen enclosing a rear patio area, formed the southern boundary.

The final terrace, to the east, consisted of three-bedroomed, single storey courtyard houses, their Z-plan form enclosing a small entrance court and patio. Ryder and Yates thus created an enclosed private development, with pedestrian access restricted to residents. The east and west sides of the site were kept open to ensure that the views to playing fields and the Tyne Valley were uninterrupted.

The elevations of all the blocks demonstrated the painterly influence of Yates, with a variety of materials, colours and finishes used to create patterns of solid and void to the walls, very much as taught by Lubetkin and as also demonstrated at Peterlee by Victor Pasmore. St Cuthbert's Green naturally echoed Ryder and Yates's earlier work at Peterlee, with flat roofs and square forms clad in render, but it also evoked Le Corbusier's housing of 1925 at Pessac, outside Bordeaux, in its use of boldly projecting units and serrated profiles. The pilot scheme resolved potential problems in these house types before the much larger housing scheme at Kenton got under way.

The North Kenton development more closely reflected government publications of the time, notably *Houses for Today and Tomorrow*, better known as the Parker Morris Report, which set minimum standards for public housing that endured through the 1960s and 1970s.[3]

Another influence was the ramifications of increased car ownership. The scheme was an organically related collection of building types, spatially subdividing the site as opposed to the more commonly used static pattern of individual, regular plots. Situated on the north-west edge of Newcastle, about three miles out, the site was connected both to the city centre and to the country, with magnificent views of the Cheviot Hills to the north.

However, there were a number of disadvantages that Ryder and Yates had to overcome. The north-facing steeply sloping site created orientation and aspect problems because the views and sunshine were on opposite sides, and had a high degree of wind exposure. The main axis ran north–south, with two plains falling away from a flat central area. School playing fields formed the eastern boundary and a proposed by-pass the western boundary, with Kenton Lane and existing housing forming the two remaining sides.

The location, and an innovative architectural style, were packaged as an up-market development of social housing where the tenants would be prepared to pay higher rents.

Three-storey flat blocks at North Kenton estate

Each house was to have an allocated garage in anticipation of the rise in car ownership, a central heating system would serve the ground floor and some of the upper floors, and thermal insulation and television aerials were designed within each dwelling so that the carefully considered roofscape would not be compromised.

The creation of a pedestrian precinct at the smaller Fenham site worked well and caused no design problems. However, on a scheme of over 600 dwellings a more complex solution had to be explored. At Kenton, a road encircled the northern and western boundaries with an exit into Kenton Lane. The housing, shops and schools were all served from spurs projecting from the main ring road, creating service and garage courts. Shorter, more pleasant routes gave separate pedestrian access to any building. The concept of a central core that housed all the public buildings, including shops, schools and a public house, was becoming less prevalent in neighbourhood thinking by the 1960s, but here it was adopted wholesale from Peterlee. It was placed at the intersection of the three main pedestrian routes, on a spur to the perimeter ring road.

Additional play space required by the brief was integrated with the existing playing fields on the eastern boundary, to help regularise the connection with older developments. Other open space was dispersed throughout the scheme to meet particular tenant demands. This was split into passive and active recreational areas, from small

Three-storey split level houses at Kenton

North Kenton estate: looking north down one of the principal promenades

areas for toddlers adjacent to dwellings, to structured play areas for older children, that extended to playing fields. Infant play areas were treated sculpturally as large playpens containing a sandpit, sheltered by shrubs, with low walls and integral seating to the remaining periphery. For junior play, permanent play objects, some treated as sculpture, were provided along the main pedestrian routes to the schools and shops. Traditional swings, slides and roundabouts were provided in carefully devised play spaces enclosed by walls and planting, with seats for parents. The playing fields were bounded on the south side by a valley of existing trees, which were supplemented with additional planting to shelter seating for spectators.

A piazza for adults was created on the upper level of the central public square with hard landscaping in the form of a fountain, pool and sculpture, with planting restricted to tree groups and small areas of flowers. In the lower level of the central area was a decorative play garden with curved pre-cast concrete screens that could be arranged to form play areas. The philosophy was that there should be no large areas of unplanted earth, with the buildings themselves completing the sculptural group, and plants providing welcome bright incidents of colour. To take advantage of the site's magnificent aspect northwards, a viewing platform, with parking and catering facilities, was provided on the high ground adjacent to Kenton Lane.

House types

The eight house and flat types were designed in accordance with Parker Morris's recommended minimum standards. They provided additional floor space, subdivided for the families' needs, and took heed of new requirements such as space for homework and hobbies, and looked at the benefits of central heating and insulation, as Ryder and Yates were quick to stress in their reports.

The development was extensively reported in the *Northern Echo*:

> Mr Ryder said, 'It will appeal to people of professional class who, for various reasons, have always been loath to go into the private builders' suburbia. They want a house to rent and the alternative has been to go into an area where properties have been reconstructed in the form of flats in Georgian and Victorian houses, which once were pleasing. We are aiming at an integrated housing estate, which will look pleasant, be attractive to live in, and also provide really first-class amenities. Although each house will have a garage, we are aiming as far as possible to eliminate the motor car from the living pattern by making one motor way and having large cul-de-sac roads.

> 'We envisage larger rooms with heat and insulation', he added. Mr Ryder said it would be the sort of house where one could play the radiogram in

one room without disturbing a child doing his homework in another. There would be central heating – either warm air or under-floor heating. 'We shall have playing spaces, and we shall retain the trees on the estate and use them in the landscaping. We shall provide a nursery, a primary school, a very small shopping centre (since the large shopping centre is at Kenton, not very far away), and there will possibly be a church. We are hoping to carry out an experiment for an absolutely new type of public house, which will really live up to its name providing amenities for the whole family and not for people who just want to drink. As we see it, this should replace the traditional community hall, which in our experience is never as fully used as it should be.'[4]

The primary school comprised eight classrooms on two floors, with infants on the ground floor, facing south over playing fields. The hall, administrative areas and kitchen were in one block enclosing the southern boundary of the main public square, and linked to the classrooms by corridors on each side of a garden court, onto which the main windows of the hall projected. The functions of the building were well defined and became an important contribution to the enclosure of the central area of the development.

A single-storey public house was designed as part of the central shopping area with public, cocktail and men-only bars, facilities that were still commonplace at that time. Each of the shops had a frontage 8 metres wide and a variable depth up to 9 metres, depending on storage requirements. The enclosed yard behind each unit opened directly onto the service road and parking area. Two-storey duplex flats were provided over each shop, with direct access to the unit if required; if the traders did not want the living accommodation, it could be made independent.

A scheme as large as North Kenton magnified any constructional problems. The contractor elected to clear all of the site topsoil in one operation, only possible because it was almost entirely free of vegetation, so construction could commence in a number of locations simultaneously. But, after foundation work had commenced, unusually heavy spring rain ran unchecked across the sloping site, making construction works very difficult.

The main contractor was very experienced with traditional house building in the area, but it would appear that the firm underestimated the innovative planning and constructional features of the Ryder and Yates scheme. Most of these problems were eventually resolved by replacing the site architect with Ted Nicklin, new to the office and who had previously worked for Sheffield City Council on the building of Park Hill; he got the construction of the Kenton scheme back on course after lengthy delays.

Ten years later, in 1974, Ryder and Yates undertook another housing project, Albany village at Washington New Town in County Durham. A housing scheme as large as that at North Kenton, Albany was completed during the years of a vernacular revival in

Housing development at Albany, Washington

Britain that emerged as a reaction to modernism's apparent failure, particularly in the realm of public housing. This approach was influential in most offices, including that of Ryder and Yates, and contributed to the confused quality of Albany.

The elevational treatment of the units at Fenham and Kenton had been a direct reference and extension to their earlier work at Peterlee, but now Ryder and Yates had to respond to a different architectural climate. After Kenton, Newcastle City Council commissioned the Sweden-based architect Ralph Erskine to rebuild the inner-city area of Byker. He and his team encouraged public participation and gave great importance to landscape design, with public, semi-public and private external spaces.

The elevations were littered with stained timber, patterned brickwork, profiled aluminium sheeting and cement fibreboard, a whole amalgam of materials in what seemed ordered chaos. It was an instant critical success and affected, directly or otherwise, contemporary housing schemes locally and nationally.

The commission for Albany therefore came at a critical period for the partnership. Construction failures at North Kenton were leading to the questioning of its flat-roof aesthetic, so important to Ryder and Yates's design philosophy. While not wanting to abandon the modernist style, it was obvious to them that, under the housing cost yardstick parameters, it was not possible to afford the sort of specification necessary to achieve any success with flat-roof technology. Ultraviolet radiation, thermal stress and condensation were other factors that now had to be considered. The uninsulated mineral roofing felts used in the standard specification for flat roofs were deemed unsuitable and just could not cope. As Ryder explained:

> I think our main problem in connection with housing is the extraordinary yardstick feeling that I think everybody has. Again this is a political matter, and if we were to be concerned about housing, we would do it a different way – we would change the politics of housing. As the politics and controls exist, we find housing the most difficult task.[5]

For the Albany development Ryder and Yates had to consider using dual pitch roofs, anathema after the struggle of the early years in which they established their basic principles. The high-density, low-rise scheme that was required could only be achieved by building half the units as flats.

The site bounded the new town centre, and the development was to be a transition zone between the traditional housing estates and the centre. The resulting development accommodated 606 dwellings at a density of 82 persons per acre, and this was only possible by making the Albany scheme as continuous as possible to reduce cost limits.

The resulting design included long banana-shaped blocks of three- and four-storey flats. The related terraced housing was grouped in pairs and organised around mixer courts – then a new planning philosophy – which integrated resident parking within landscape on one side of the terrace and pedestrian access only on the remaining side. This was a result of research at the Kenton scheme, which showed tenant dissatisfaction with long walks to the garage courts away from dwellings.

By extending the roof tiling down the fenestration to first-floor level, a form of pitched roof aesthetic was achieved that was acceptable to Ryder and Yates's tastes. The covering was a multi-coloured interlocking concrete tile, which contrasted with dark brown brickwork and stained timber pergolas. Tenants were involved in the design of pergolas in the form of screens or fencing as a framework for extension to personalise their space, and the integral garages to the narrow-fronted houses were designed to be converted easily to additional rooms.

The Development Corporation was also interested in adopting a block or neighbourhood heating scheme, and research by the practice showed that gas at that time was comparatively cheap. This led to the creation of a small boiler room to each court supplying all the heating needs of the housing.

Fundamental changes in government housing policies, particularly with tenants' rights to buy, have compromised both the Fenham and the Kenton developments and led to inappropriate changes, as they have to social housing everywhere. St Cuthbert's

Green has had some remodelling, notably with the introduction of pitched roofs, but Kenton has survived remarkably well, save for replacement doors and windows. Unfortunately, however, Albany has suffered from sheer neglect.

Notes

1   Gordon Ryder, letter, 1 February 1994, Ryder papers.
2   *Northern Architect*, no. 1, November 1961, p3.
3   Ministry of Housing and Local Government, circular no. 13/62, *Homes for Today and Tomorrow*, London, HMSO, 1962.
4   'Top people's rents for new estate', *Northern Echo*, Friday, 17 January 1964.
5   Gordon Ryder, *RIBA Journal*, vol. 83, no. 1, January 1976, p28.

Veduta di una Citta, Peter Yates, c.1952

CHAPTER FIVE:
Exhibition Design

As well as houses, the 1950s saw Ryder and Yates produce a series of exhibition stands, mostly for subsidiaries of the British Plaster and Boards Company. They were given a free rein for decorative and informative themes to be explored to the full, while the small scale and impermanence of the stands enabled the architects to break down the barriers and limitations of design and dispel their inhibitions: 'a marvellous training ground for sculpture and colour – everything we wanted to do. You can do anything with an exhibition stand.'[1]

In this they were following a familiar course taken by modernists since the 1920s, when trade stands and exhibition pavilions mapped the course of the new architecture with seminal designs by Le Corbusier and Mies van der Rohe. The need to attract attention and generate excitement encouraged experiments with new shapes and volumes, and Ryder and Yates established a design vocabulary. It was not just a visual catalogue of shapes but a process of refining a design to its simplest form and adding appendages to create interest. This would be fundamental to their later design methodology. Ryder and Yates found:

> To convince a client that to get one idea across in terms of building and display is an achievement. Against a background of every conceivable lighting display, building materials and colour arrangement, and the overbearing structure of the Olympia exhibition hall, a way must be found to ensure recognition.[2]

The design for the first exhibition stand for Carlite Plaster – a product of the Carlisle Plaster and Cement Company, part of British Plaster and Boards – was begun in 1952, before the partnership of Ryder and Yates was formed. Peter Yates was involved in its construction at Olympia in 1953, but although the stand was dramatic and functional, it was not as sophisticated as later designs, probably because his input was limited. At that time Yates was also designing exhibition stands in Paris.

All the components of the stand, walls, roof and the central sculptural shape, were formed from fibrous plaster. The elegant central form contained a contra-rotating plaster bag and a trowel embedded in a plaster whorl. High-intensity lighting cast a strong, changing shadow pattern on the inner white wall of the plaster shape. A reinforced plaster symbol was designed to be completely self-supporting, but two metal wires were fixed at the last minute as a result of a general lack of faith in scientific

Exhibition stand for Carlite Plaster at Olympia, 1953

calculation. Hollow plaster bags on the stand's sidewall, internally illuminated, displayed photographs of various types of buildings. The largely white stand was enlivened with contrasting walls of dark green and red, while the sculptural quality of the three-dimensional lettering crowning its roof made it similar to that used by Lubetkin for the entrance to Bevin Court.

The next Carlite stand at Olympia, in 1957, benefited from Yates's greater experience of exhibition work. He refined the design to three symbolic shapes: cone, rhomboid and square, set on a rectilinear base. The grouping, a juxtaposition of primary forms that would inform all their subsequent work, was formed from plaster, and was repeated three times in a diminishing order. This elegant and apparently minimalist statement disguised a complex structural system beneath its simpler surfaces, a recurring theme in their later work, with the fibrous plaster as matrix, and stainless steel as reinforcement.

Exhibition stand for Carlite Plaster at Olympia, 1957

Gotham stand highlighting Carlite Plaster, 1959

Smooth, white, cool and perfectly plaster-like, the tall slender cone and the plaster rhomboid were mounted on a plaster sheathed steel frame. Note the long counter desk sitting on an exciting floor pattern of multi-coloured silk-screened felt.[3]

Lighting was dramatic, ensuring both illumination and recognition. The base of the stand was covered in a myriad of silk-screened felt panels containing the trade names and colours of the company, in what became a familiar Ryder and Yates presentation style. The *Builder*'s reporter was impressed:

I nearly missed a little gem … with its tall slender cone, the little penthouse aloft, peopled by hundreds of little figures (on a photo mural) 'going over to Carlite'. Would I have tried a red ceiling on this little house? A clever arrangement of raw materials at eye level and a long graceful counter desk

sitting easily on an almost-too-exciting floor pattern. Slick and sophisticated – or are these the wrong words for such a pure display? And one of
the most economic, I'll warrant.[4]

The 1959 exhibition stand for the Gotham group of companies, who, like the Carlisle
Plaster and Cement Company, would become part of British Gypsum, was again
dramatic, original and highly symbolic. The platform, or counter, was black, while a
single column of white reinforced plaster supported a cantilevered superstructure
overhead.

From within the two revolving cubes occulting spotlights scan the exhibit,
producing a constantly changing progression of light and shadow that will
virtually never repeat. Inexhaustible possibilities of textural plaster panels
under different lighting conditions. The counter top, a single mirror 20 feet
by 5, multiplies the movement, shape and lights. A cube hung at eye level by
two threads was tumbled by an internal mechanism. The faces of the cube,
with contrasting colours, photos and numbers, describe the versatility of
plaster.[5]

Because of their very temporary nature, with one exception, we have to rely on
reports of the time for visitors' impressions of these stands. George Grenfell Baines,
writing in the *Builder*, penned a typical reaction:

First on my list for everything – visual appeal, telling the story, good
colour, lettering, lighting, wit and humour – comes the Gotham Group
of Companies' stand. Plaster is their business, and aren't those four flying
wing walls poised from a sculptured central tower ravishingly textured
– one with pebble-like protuberances, one with sharp, clean-cut crystalline
cantilevers, one with clusters of cylinders, and one with, I forget what,
though I will never forget the brilliant lighting effects, some from moving
sources which, hidden inside huge revolving cubes, cast ever-varying lights
and shadows on these exciting white forms. As I was saying, aren't those
four flying walls eloquent of the thing they are supposed to be? – plaster.
It made me realise what a lovely, satisfying material this is, in spite of the
wetness and the shortness of labour. The long flow of the centre counter,
with a simple check plastic fascia posed well above the top holding a
'Toblerone' type sign with a message cleverly printed on the bottom face
so that you read it in the mirror top like a sly aside from [Tony] Hancock.
Yes, this stand had everything, including a very attractive girl who did not,
of course, notice me. Still, I've come away to specify plaster again, so what
more can I say?[6]

An extended brief for British Gypsum in 1962 called for a trade pavilion that
would be exposed to outside elements, with stands and displays within it. It thus came

to resemble a small building in the International Style, with a white facade, ribbon windows, flat roof and slender columns. The sophisticated structural system consisted of perimeter steel columns with lattice girders – likened by Yates to those of the Crystal Palace – to span the office space without the need for intermediate support.

Formica-faced timber panels and aluminium glazing were hung on the outside of the expressed columns to form the envelope for the new building. After the exhibition the stand, like those before it, was demolished, but the engineer Leszek Kubik, working for Ryder and Yates, negotiated the purchase of the steel frame from the contractors for reuse in the practice's own offices at Killingworth.

British Gypsum stand, 1962. Main elevation

Notes

1   Peter Yates, 'Architects' approach to Architecture', *Architects' Journal*, vol. 162, no. 46, 12 November 1975, p993.
2   Gordon Ryder and Peter Yates, 'Designing for the exhibition', *Northern Architect*, no. 4, May 1962, p66.
3   Ibid. p68.
4   G. Grenfell Baines, 'Olympian Glades', *Builder*, vol. 193, no. 5983, November 1957, p955.
5   Ryder and Yates, *Northern Architect*, no. 4, op. cit., p69.
6   G. Grenfell Baines, 'Olympia Revisited' *Builder*, vol. 197, no. 6081, December 1959, p796.

CHAPTER SIX:
Refurbishment

Martins Bank appointed Ryder and Yates after Mr Walton, its northern director, read Anne Glidewell's appreciative article in the *Daily Express* on the Liddell House in Tynemouth and felt that they were the architects to revitalise the bank's image in the region. 'He said it was about time something happened to the design of our banks,' Ryder explained. 'We then reconstructed part of the interior of Martins banks in Grey Street Newcastle and in Hexham.'[1]

This led to a number of refit schemes, which were important in promoting the work of the practice. The abstract and cool facades by Ryder and Yates presented a direct confrontation with the classical architecture and historical locations of the banks, a complete contrast that was crucial to their success. The refurbishment of Martins Bank in Hexham, in 1962, showed a respect for the original, classically inspired facade, but a remodelled ground floor including a dramatic insertion in the form of a main entrance entirely of glass. The Edwardian interior was comprehensively upgraded to include a less formal banking hall, which included a mural by Peter Yates on a historical subject.

One of the bank's regular customers was Dr Burns, the chairman of the Northern Gas Board, who would later commission Ryder and Yates to design new headquarters in Killingworth, and recommended them for a whole series of buildings for the gas industry.

The language of the trade stands was transferred to a series of commercial refits in the centre of Newcastle, beginning in 1962. For a firm of opticians, F. Robson and Co. in Pilgrim Street, a facade was designed almost entirely of 19-millimetre clear plate glass, and the plastic-laminate-faced plywood panels were engraved with the company's name. Although the original Victorian shopfront and reception area were replaced in this refit, the remainder of the ground and upper floors remained unchanged. The small reception area was modelled almost entirely in white Formica-faced panels, and adjoining the main entrance was a black screen, also of Formica, that depicted a map of the medieval layout of the area of Newcastle in which the shop stood. The advantage of using Formica was that it could accept the introduction of artwork, patterns and signing into its finish. Ryder and Yates promoted the technique over many years in conjunction with the American manufacturer of Formica at its factory in nearby North Shields. The shop received a Civic Trust Commendation in 1963. The facade lasted into the 1990s, a remarkable achievement given the expected

Opposite: Blue Boat, Greece, Peter Yates, c.1979

Peter Yates with the manager of Martins Bank, Hexham

life cycle for plastic laminates and for shopfronts generally. It has been replaced with an all-glass facade.

The refurbishment of the head office of the Northern Counties Permanent Building Society in Market Street, Newcastle, in 1964, included a new banking hall and offices. There was also a new facade to Market Street, comprising two large display windows linked with the main entrance. These windows, used to promote goods and services, had a 'floating facade' constructed from Formica and glass, but the apparently straight-forward design hid a complex structure of steelwork to achieve the desired effect. The stonework framing the main window was painted black to complement the smoke-stained buildings of the surrounding city centre.

Some years later, for a second phase of development, Ryder and Yates proposed a solid-faced elevation that incorporated the Society's new name (after they had amalga-mated with the Rock Building Society), Northern Rock, set in storey-high letters of glass-fibre reinforced plastic adjacent to the original display cabinets. By contrast, the corner of the building turning into Pilgrim Street was transformed with a revolving glass door. This presented the main banking hall to the street, and was set with an illustration depicting Newcastle's main thoroughfare in medieval times, blown up to a large scale and screen-printed onto white Formica. Ryder and Yates also undertook refurbishments of the Society's offices in St Mary's Place in the north of Newcastle, and at Gateshead and Carlisle.

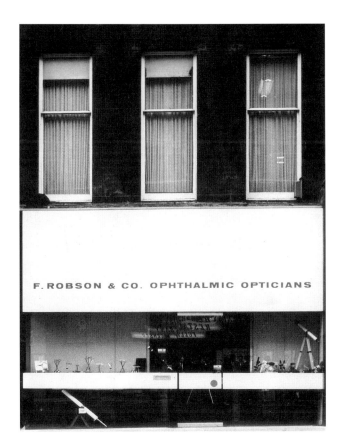

F. Robson and Co., Pilgrim Street, Newcastle

Northern Counties Permanent Building Society, Market Street, Newcastle

Notes

1   Gordon Ryder, quoted in *Northern Echo*, Thursday, 18 November, 1971.

CHAPTER SEVEN:
Building for the Gas Industry

The commercial series of buildings by Ryder and Yates had, by their very brief and scale, a different range of design parameters and themes from the earlier domestic projects. However, the language developed for the private houses was not discarded but was extended, with Peter Yates bringing to these large stages a still greater theatricality. At Killingworth, the location of their major buildings for the gas industry, Ryder and Yates sought to create a sense of place, to make an architectural response to a brand new landscape in a bleak area of derelict mineshafts. This they achieved by a series of metaphors in the form of horns, towers and ceremonial entrances, amid other dramatic incidents. These evolved out of ideas initiated in the houses and exhibition stands, the latter by their very nature over-dramatic. In fact, all Ryder and Yates's buildings, including housing schemes, included gestures in the design that drew attention to the architecture.

Such gestures were not confined, however, to artistic symbols but ran through the building in the choice of materials and the use of technology. This is important because Ryder and Yates always worked closely with engineers, although it was only from 1963 that they could afford to run a multi-disciplinary practice. Thereafter engineers took a greater role, and the practice's architectural vocabulary expanded.

After the small domestic commissions, the larger scale of Ryder and Yates's first commercial buildings inevitably required new structural techniques. Clients demanded offices and workshops uncluttered by any evidence of structure, and no columns or beams were allowed to obstruct the internal planning of these critical areas, ensuring their complete flexibility. The result was an architecture of facade and structure, particularly well seen in the earlier projects such as Patterson's garage and their first offices for the gas industry.

All manner of structural systems were explored, utilised and pushed to the limit. Technology was re-explored or invented, and materials – new and traditional – were used in fresh and innovative ways. Their sense of planning may have initially been indebted to Lubetkin's marriage of a precise form to a specific brief, but Ryder and Yates went much further with their commercial designs to meet new and more indeterminate challenges, as many of the buildings were without precedent or even a clear brief, and required an original outlook.

Opposite: Britain, Peter Yates, c.1953

Norgas House viewed from across the lake

The buildings had, by definition, to be commercially viable, but had also to present a corporate or fresh image and to create appropriate environments for people to work or shop in. Environmental considerations had to be explored in greater detail with the design of heating, ventilation and air-conditioning systems, and it was important for the practice to understand the effects of solar gain and the special atmospheric requirements needed for specific machinery or processes. Maintenance on all the buildings had to be kept to an absolute minimum and this in turn affected the choice of materials and their application.

In the 1960s, the city of Newcastle upon Tyne led by its charismatic leader T. Dan Smith and with Wilfred Burns as City Planning Officer no less controversial in his way, entrusted its three major central schemes to Basil Spence, Robert Matthew and Arne Jacobsen.[1] However, many commentators felt that local architects should be given the opportunity to design a prestige building in the city centre. This was highlighted by the problems experienced by the Northern Gas Board, which had intended to build its new headquarters in the city, where it was already established. Delays imposed while Burns was preparing his central plan led it to choose a site at Killingworth, a new town being developed seven miles to the north.[2]

The new township was first proposed in 1959 by Northumberland County Council as a means of regenerating a former area of open-cast coal mining, and it was developed in the 1960s under the guidance of Roy Gazzard, who had been chief planner at Peterlee and was familiar with the work of Ryder and Yates. Yates described taking the chairman, Dr J. Burns, to see 'a no-man's land. The mines had gone leaving a flat waste, a sunken pit flash flooded where a slough had subsided, a few pigeon houses and a floating dead pig. He was not deterred.'[3]

The Northern Gas Board wanted a first-class modern headquarters that would not be out of date 25 years hence. It decided as a matter of policy to employ a local architect, whom it chose in 1963 from a list of six proposed by Professor Jack Napper, Head of the School of Architecture. The selection of an architect from a shortlist prepared by a senior academic figure was a method often used in the 1950s and 1960s, many clients preferring it to a competition as they could make their own choice rather than having to abide by that of the RIBA. After looking at examples of their work, including the refurbishment of Martins Bank in Hexham, the Gas Board chose Ryder and Yates. Freddie Green, Secretary to the Board, subsequently wrote: 'I'm glad we did. This policy of flying to Basil Spence cuts no ice with us. Firms which have gone outside will be lucky if they get as good a job as we did.'[4]

Norgas House site layout

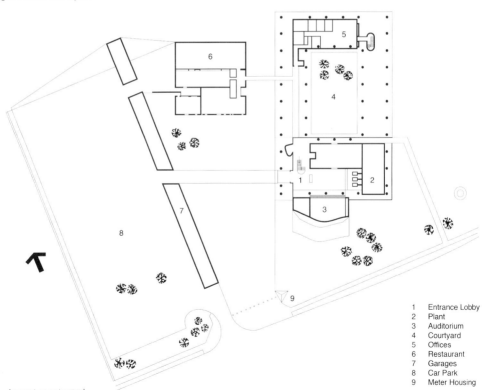

1	Entrance Lobby
2	Plant
3	Auditorium
4	Courtyard
5	Offices
6	Restaurant
7	Garages
8	Car Park
9	Meter Housing

It was the architects' first large project, then valued at £750,000.

Newcastle's loss became Killingworth's gain, with the headquarters building, Norgas House, providing the key to bringing other industry to the township. It became home to the Ryder and Yates office, and the location for many of their best-known buildings. The practice found an enlightened client in Northern Gas under the chairmanship of Dr Burns, who gave it the opportunity to build significantly. The Northern Gas Board was a committee made up of local businessmen and experts to oversee the running of the gas industry in the north.

Norgas House, completed in 1965, and the Gas Council's Engineering Research Station, finished in 1967, represented the high point of the practice's output and gained them national status through a series of architectural awards. Their design vocabulary was now fully developed and was applied to buildings of significant scale. Both buildings were precise in their relationship with the newly restored landscape, a flat site on the south side of a great artificial lake formed from the flooded slough.

The ample space available and the client's requirements for maximum flexibility led to a horizontal format, in which all the offices were located on two floors around a central courtyard or 'secret garden', the lower floor being raised on columns or pilotis above ground level, which was left open save for the entrance hall, reception and plant rooms. The office space was designed on a 1.6-metre-square module that permitted

Roof lights in the form of Minoan horns over the restaurant block

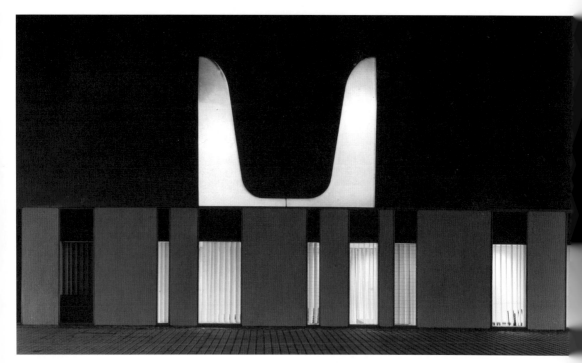

demountable partitions for flexible space planning. Only the boardroom suite and toilet accommodation were fixed. Additionally a small private auditorium for lectures and seminars, with 100 seats, was provided next to the main entrance. Restaurant facilities, together with a caretaker's flat, were provided in a separate single-storey block linked to the main building by a glazed walkway and expressed by an upstanding roof light made of fibreglass and shaped in the form of the Minoan horns of Knossos.

The need for maximum flexibility restricted the number and placing of structural columns on the upper floors, while the high level of servicing that was required for air conditioning, computers, telephones and electrical services necessitated an accessible service floor to be incorporated. The use of a curtain wall system for the upper floors was one of the first in the North and consisted of glazing and vitreous steel spandrel panels set in full-height aluminium frames, fully insulated and designed to be cleaned from a roof-suspended cradle. To avoid the horizontal dictates of fire-stop walls between floors these were designed in the form of more steel panels. Although these fire-stop walls did not create a design aesthetic, they are clearly visible as a dark grey infill between the storey-high curtain wall panels, amid a dominant vertical pattern to the main facade, termed by the architects a 'giant order' just like those used by Palladio to pull together a rectangular composition.[5]

For a building of the early 1960s Norgas House was a very sophisticated design in its servicing. This included a full air-conditioning system for the main block, warm-air heating to the restaurant block, and under-slab heating to the external concrete entrance court to prevent ice forming in winter. The requirement for the building to advertise the use of gas was cleverly met by exposing the boiler house, adjacent to the main entrance, by means of glass walls so that its three gas boilers were visible from both inside and out. The expression of the service towers on the roof was also rationalised to produce a formal sculpture to the skyline, together with the name of the building in giant letters.

Ryder and Yates designed a flexible partitioning system, but failed to patent it, something they later regretted when it was picked up by other firms. Its use imposed a rigid discipline on the electrical layout, with fluorescent tubes set in modular bays giving a high level of illumination whatever the chosen office format. Telephone and electrical power points were similarly set in the floor to suit the modular layout. Two cordless telephone switchboards were provided adjacent to the main entrance in a glass enclosure, together with an automatic dictation system and staff location transmitters.

From commission to the completion of the building took less than two years, timed to meet the delivery of the computer system. By lifting the building on columns there was the possibility of making additional space below, in separate units that could be added or removed as required. Yates likened Norgas House to 'a jellyfish capable of extending down and out in all direction and as hurriedly contracting'. In 1965 expansion was not on the agenda, but two years later the ground floor began to be enclosed as more staff were employed, both to cater for an increased use of gas and for developing their use of computing.

Norgas House

To keep it clearly subservient to the main building, the restaurant group beyond the glass link was set into the ground, while its horn-like roof lights gave it a separate identity. The unusual form of the horns, with their boat-like section, led the builders to prefabricate them on site from fibreglass using marine technology. Fibreglass was used because it was a flexible material able to take any form, and was translucent, lightweight and relatively inexpensive.

The use of sculptural forms continued with a pyramid set at the entrance to the site, which housed a giant gas meter with each face a different colour and set slightly apart to induce airflow. A cooling cascade for the air conditioning was an outlying feature in the landscape, made from a cylinder of green glass panels set above a pool. This sculptural theme was carried through internally with the cantilevered form of the main stair, the boilers, and a reception desk and foundation stone placed to subdivide the entrance spaces. Peter Yates explained that they had wanted "'to refine a building so that it becomes completely non-representational and abstract": all the accepted vocabulary is re-examined, rejected or very carefully refined until it is abstract; this is not perverse, nature consists of these simple elements.'[6]

The Minoan horns were removed in a comprehensive refurbishment of the building in the early 1990s, together with the boardroom suite, the main staircase and other internal features. Northern Gas was thus able to successfully challenge proposals that it should be listed. It is now only partly occupied by its successor, the National Grid, and the building is at risk.

It is important to consider Norgas House in conjunction with the Engineering Research Station, which was completed two years later on a nearby site. Here the client was British Gas, rather than the locally controlled Northern Gas. It is Ryder and Yates's best-known building, with its uncompromising design and clarity of form producing a piece of pure architecture.

The original brief rather long-windedly described the Research Station as 'research and development into engineering and metallurgy to service distribution in the gas industry'. The director, David van der Post, had six scientists when he commissioned the building, but two years later he would have 200. He therefore wanted 'a playpen for boffins', with 'everything on view – there would be no scientists tucked in corners or going off in their own direction'.

There were no precedents for a building of this type in the United Kingdom, but examination of similar laboratories in the United States, such as Eero Saarinen's Bell Research Center, designed in 1957, showed that open-plan facilities could be provided economically. However, during the initial stages of the design, natural gas was discovered in large quantities under the North Sea. As a result, the British Gas Council

Photomontage of Ryder and Yates buildings in Killingworth

could not give the architects a firm brief, since it was impossible to predict the direction of future research and development. It asked for the provision of offices, a canteen, and laboratories and a workshop capable of accommodating unpredictable activities.

Two major requirements for the new building emerged. There was a need first for rapid physical growth in the whole structure, and second for flexibility in the laboratory area to meet alterations to the research programme and arrival of new disciplines. Ryder and Yates's solution was a fixed area containing offices, the canteen and car park, and a wholly modular and extendable element containing laboratories and workshops set off a central spine. A separate wing contained a store for dangerous chemicals and a testing bay.

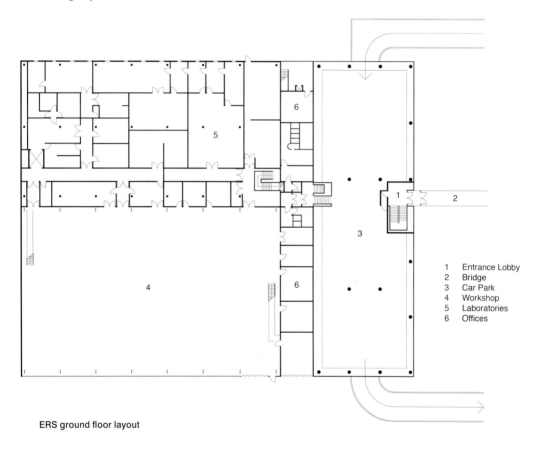

1	Entrance Lobby
2	Bridge
3	Car Park
4	Workshop
5	Laboratories
6	Offices

ERS ground floor layout

The fixed element, comprising the offices, canteen and library, set over two levels of car parking, had a concrete structure and was firmly anchored to the landscape with a series of highly sculptural roof towers. These towers, three venturi-shaped and three cylindrical, contained water tanks and extract flues. They were lifted onto the roof by the two largest cranes in the country, pushing crane technology of the time to its limit. During their construction the local press was fascinated by the collection of 'way out' concrete shapes on the forecourt of a new £500,000 building at Killingworth new town [that] have really led the public astray. Motorists and travellers passing the new Engineering Research Station being built there for the Gas Research Council of Great Britain, were puzzled by the shapes, some rounded, some conical and all of them up to 26 feet high. Most popular conclusion – that it was all part of some modern mural decoration for the building. Next month, however, that theory will be blown 'sky high'. All the shapes will end up on the roof, more than seventy feet above the road. The shapes include two new towers, each built to contain twenty tons of water, and extractor units.[7]

Gordon Ryder explained that:

All modern complex buildings have these sorts of shapes on the roof, and we have designed them to fit in with what is a very modern building … The whole building has been designed so that it can be portioned off into different-sized areas, according to need. The contract is worth more than £500,000, and it's the biggest outside the London area.[8]

For the extendable part of the building – an air-conditioned hangar housing the laboratories and workshops – Ryder and Yates turned to steel construction as the most flexible response to the nebulous brief. On one side of the extendable spine was a double-height workshop for big rigs and, on the other, two storeys of offices and

ERS roof towers

laboratories, those on the upper level opening off the spine and designed to encourage workers in the three sections to communicate with each other.

A specially designed partitioning system was adopted, which incorporated all the services in triple demountable ducts leading from a service deck in the virendeel roof, in much the same way as in Norgas House. Designed as a kit of parts, it was assembled in an ongoing discussion as the research heads arrived just three months before the building opened.

Externally, the Engineering Research Station (ERS) was clad in module-wide pre-cast concrete panels, incorporating heating and ventilation ducts. These panels were painted to ensure a unity of finish as the building was later extended and, more importantly, to give homogeneity to the fixed and flexible elements of the building. The panels, together with an uninterrupted ribbon of glazing, gave the exterior a formality which the indeterminate nature of its rear part belied. The client wanted the impression of order and organisation to be presented to the visitor, both externally and internally, whatever the agreed layout: the chosen aesthetic, complete with funnels, was reminiscent of an ocean liner in the best modernist tradition.

The planned extension zone on the rear facade was clad in steel panels, which could be removed with minimum disturbance to the building or the workforce. Flexibility was always important to Ryder and Yates, but never more so than here. In the ERS, the client was able to use a kit of parts to determine the planning of a major part of the building, something that eluded most designers. The building was subsequently doubled in length, but at the fifth stage of planned extension it was decided that an intended School of Engineering should be housed in a separate structure.

Artwork was always an important element in the design vocabulary of Ryder and Yates, whether in creating an image, giving information or being purely decorative. Here, however, Yates was not given the opportunity to create a mural; instead, the building achieved an artistic effect with its distinctive groupings of roof motifs and earth sculpture – half mounds on either side of an entrance bridge extended vertically to first-floor level, but cut away in front of the car park and supported on structural retaining walls. The bridge was denoted by a free-standing square arch. 'The earth rises and breathes, like a human breast, demonstrating the two great problems of architecture, how to bring a building up out of the ground and how to finish it on top.'[9] The mounds also had the effect of screening the two levels of car parking and disguising the overall height of the building.

The *Sunday Times* called the new laboratory 'an unforgettable landmark in the Northumberland new town of Killingworth'.[10] It was officially opened by Reginald Freeson MP in December 1968, and won the Financial Times Award for Industrial Architecture the same year. The *Sunday Times* further suggested that, together with the headquarters of the Northern Gas Board and the first part of the town centre or Citadel, 'the laboratory is one of three spectacular "cathedrals of technology" which dominate the town – all of them by the same Newcastle University [sic] trained architects'.

The article also suggested that 'the laboratory's exterior is a rare case of the

Stephenson House, Killingworth

exuberant expression of modern technology in sculpturally exciting form. The interior, reflecting all the imponderables of research in the era of North Sea gas, is one of the most flexible ever created, with special partitioning designed by the architects themselves and now taken up commercially by a manufacturer. Designed six months before the discovery of North Sea gas, the building has been able to meet the demands of new research.'

Like Norgas House and the other buildings for the gas industry, the ERS has been affected by the change in the role of its statutory organisations, and was vacated in 1995. North Tyneside Council then took it on, but in 2008 it was again empty. The building was listed Grade II* in January 1997.

Stephenson House, a speculative office building designed for the Northern Gas Board Trustees for multi-occupation, was constructed in 1969 on a site opposite Norgas House and was named in honour of the railway pioneer George Stephenson, who moved to Killingworth in 1804. The design was a simple two-storey block but, like Norgas House, it was elevated off the ground on columns around a central courtyard.

The main approach from the car park to the west was by a flight of steps, extending the full length of the building and descending into a brick-lined entrance court with a central blue mosaic pool. From this area five points of entry were available, either by

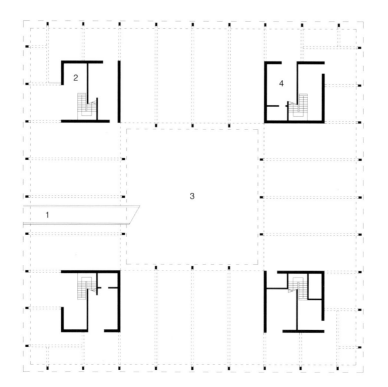

1   Entrance
2   Stair Well
3   Courtyard
4   Service Cores

Stephenson House layout

stairs contained in the four corner service towers, or centrally by a ramp bridging the pool. The offices were devised on a 1.2-metre grid, setting the pattern for the structure and a fenestration of heavy concrete panels serving as heating ducts.

The speculative nature of the building meant that there was no budget for air-conditioning, and the decision to have a less sophisticated heating and ventilating system was a major factor governing the building's design. Heavy, dense materials were used, designed to react slowly to temperature changes, with windows reduced to deeply recessed strip glazing to prevent solar gain.

Stephenson House chronologically followed the ERS, and although very different in concept, its visual form followed that building's alternative solid and void aesthetic. However, in organisational terms it more closely followed Norgas House, with its square doughnut format – the central open courtyard reducing the depth of the plan and allowing natural lighting to all the office spaces. Almost certainly because of its low-cost, speculative remit, Stephenson House lacked many of the sculptural and metaphorical features of Norgas House and the ERS. However, its competent and straightforward design carried on their architectural vocabulary. Its speculative nature and range of tenants has ensured it has remained more or less as built.

Stephenson House, Killingworth

A training college for Northern Gas, built in 1971, occupied an important location at one of the entrances into Killingworth, and the local planners were keen to ensure that the building was appropriately prestigious in appearance. The brief was to provide instruction and training facilities for the Gas Board's employees. It was refined to four basic elements: lecture rooms and offices, workshops, a canteen, and an external training compound.

The lecture rooms, offices and workshops were all expected to require later expansion and were therefore grouped together in a single-storey rectilinear block capable of vertical extension. The canteen and plant rooms, which were to remain fixed, were in a separate block linked by a glazed corridor. The enclosure that this corridor formed was treated as the main entrance, with the elevated entry flanked by blue mosaic-lined pools in much the same way as the entrance to Norgas House.

The building is a single-storey construction using an exposed steel portal frame with brick infill panels. Ryder and Yates took the opportunity to experiment with technology by designing the college to take extra floors, and they exposed and expressed the steel structural frame on the facade of the building. By setting the ground floor back from the structural line, it became independent of the main framework so that any additions would not affect the existing building. Thus the framework gave a unity to the envelope of the complex, and was matched by the module of the boundary fence. The open-sided compound for external training was covered with a proprietary space deck, a galvanised

Northern Gas Training College, Killingworth

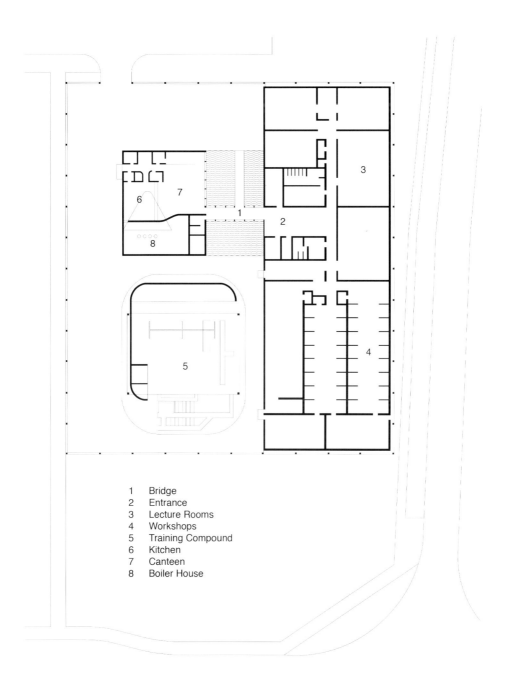

1   Bridge
2   Entrance
3   Lecture Rooms
4   Workshops
5   Training Compound
6   Kitchen
7   Canteen
8   Boiler House

Northern Gas Training College layout

steel structure system similar to that which they had earlier used in an extension for used cars at R. H. Patterson in Newcastle.

The training college was located, like many of the buildings in Killingworth, on a partly cleared site containing ventilation shafts and underground galleries from the old mine workings. The main coal shaft was rafted over; other cavities were bridged or filled with concrete. However, there remained the possibility of further subterranean hazards which, together with the extendible design, necessitated a structure of pin-based steel portal frames. This system made any subsequent frames easy to connect as well as allowing for remedial action in the event of local failure; it also permitted last-minute modifications on site.

Whereas the problem of matching materials in future building extensions was solved at ERS by painting the concrete panels, for the training centre a hard blue brindle engineering brick was used. This brick was also used internally as a facing material in the communal areas, where its hard, uncompromising finish was perfect for the rough treatment handed out by the students.

All the other external materials, including the steel structure, metal screen, space frame, the louvred screens to plant rooms and the external doors, related in their grey colour to the blue brickwork. Even the flush-fitting, dark grey solar glazing to the class-rooms was designed to be read as one with the facade. There was no entrance arch or

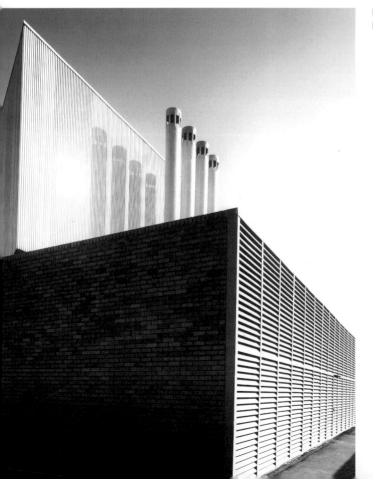

Northern Gas Training College, Killingworth

Norgas computer building, Killingworth

canopy to the training centre, but the roofscape was treated in a dramatic and interesting way. The separate plant room had a facade of louvred steel panels, with tanks and flues at roof level set back and enclosed in vertically ribbed panelling. This tank enclosure was parabolic in plan with flues extending from the plant room in front of it, giving a simple but highly sculptural roof form.

Like its predecessors, this building has fallen victim to the reorganisation of Northern Gas. A computer services company now occupies the college, and its conversion from a training facility to an office building has resulted in changes to its internal organisation and subsequently to the fenestration.

Norgas House was designed to accommodate 400–600 staff in 1963, but it was later envisaged that increased mechanisation would reduce the numbers by 200. Accordingly it was intended that the ground-floor additions would be removed to leave a two-storey building raised on columns. However, the discovery of North Sea gas and the subsequent massive conversion programme increased the workload, and the Gas Board found that installing more computers did not reduce staff numbers. Consequently a separate computer centre was built alongside, completed in 1974. Designed with a link to Norgas House containing storage bays, it was a single-storey structure 47 metres square on plan, but designed for extension by up to three storeys.

Norgas computer building layout

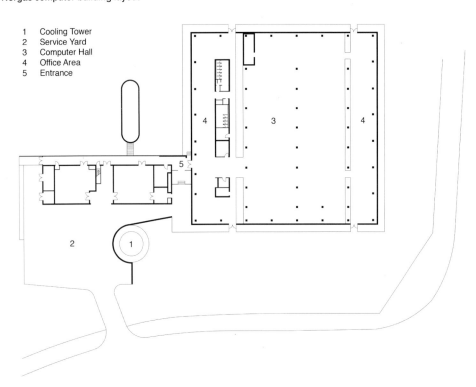

1   Cooling Tower
2   Service Yard
3   Computer Hall
4   Office Area
5   Entrance

Norgas computer building, Killingworth

A completely glazed structure provided internal flexibility by allowing partitions to be placed almost anywhere. There was an outer skin of reflective glass, a cavity, and then an inner skin of insulating and heat-absorbing material that formed the modular frame for the windows. The glazed outer skin and partially glazed inner skin, together with the necessary cavity, acted as a thermal wall to reduce energy requirements in a heavily serviced building. Moreover, its light- and heat-reflecting properties provided an effective contrast to Norgas House, in the way that other 'mirror glass' buildings across the country responded to their neighbours.

Ryder and Yates imported a partially distorted mirror glazing system from Corning Glass in Pittsburgh, and set it in exposed aluminium framing to bring a rectilinear order to the facade. It remains as built, apart from the replacement of some glazed panels with those of a different reflective tint, but its long-term fate is closely linked to that of its neighbour Norgas House.

The School of Engineering, constructed alongside the original Engineering Research Station, also in 1974, was created for the teaching of new techniques in the distribution of natural gas. The design for the School of Engineering comprised classrooms, workshops, a formal lecture theatre and a restaurant that supplemented facilities in the main building.

Although this new building was within 8 metres of the Research Station and physically linked by an aerial glass walkway, its form and materials were entirely different.

School of Engineering, Killingworth, east elevation

School of Engineering floor plan

1 Bridge / Entrance
2 Auditorium
3 Exhibition Space
4 Dining
5 Servery
6 Staff Canteen
7 Kitchen

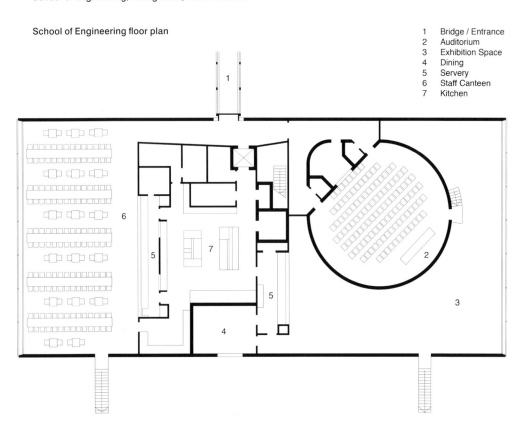

School of Engineering: south elevation

The external walls were still of pre-cast concrete panels, but the module was different and the surface finish was an exposed aggregate of broken brown glass rather than the acrylic paint of the original. The aggregate in the panels was complemented in the glazing by the use of bronze-tinted anti-sun glass.

The two flush-fitting fire escape doors on the southern facade were given the same aggregate facing as the concrete panels which, together with the partial glass enclosure to the external stairs, meant that they did not disrupt the rhythm of the facade. A young assistant was asked to detail these 'invisible staircases', but his response of a blank drawing sheet did not amuse Gordon Ryder.

On-line Inspection Centre, Cramlington

OLI, Cramlington: office building

The School of Engineering, like the ERS, hid its structure behind a formal facade, but here the rectilinear envelope concealed a circular lecture theatre. The enclosure of this circular construction within the rectilinear box necessitated, yet again, a highly original and complex engineering structure, comprising a suspended horseshoe beam to support the lecture theatre and allow circulation underneath.

As at the ERS the impact of the building was reduced by setting it behind earth sculpture. This building was also vacated in early 2008 by North Tyneside Metropolitan District Council, but is covered by the listing of ERS.

The On-line Inspection Centre (OLI) at Cramlington, built in 1979, was unique in Ryder and Yates's work in that it was located within the shell of an existing building, a solution that produced great economies for British Gas, not only in cost but also in time. The building was a former Courtaulds weaving shed, of two broad bays with a pitched, double-gabled roof. However, British Gas was aware of the modern image created by the highly successful Research Station and wanted to impart something of this to the older building.

It was needed for the manufacture of one-tonne electrical robots, a development of an idea first explored at the ERS for a so-called 'intelligent pig' that would travel through the pipelines identifying faults and corrosion. The large uninterrupted floor area of the former weaving sheds, naturally top lit, was perfect for the mass production of these robots, an operation that was outgrowing ERS. Basing production at Cramlington, a short distance away from the main British Gas headquarters, perhaps also made it easier to market the product to customers outside the gas industry, including operatives of other pipeline distribution systems such as the oil and water service industries.

By the construction of a new office and computer complex, linked by a glass corridor to the existing factory halfway across its facade, the great visual mass of the sheds was broken up. A circular entrance court in front of this glass link, similar to that at the Norgas Training College, and a glass-fronted restaurant in front of the exposed twin gables, completed the accommodation and introduced a formal modern imagery.

The east nave retained its full height and operated as a workshop and crane bay, while the west, which was attached to the new buildings, had a lowered ceiling, with plant and services incorporated into the resulting void. An additional system of horizontal oval windows inside the original fenestration created 'thermal walls', similar to those for the computer building at Norgas House, to achieve the controlled environment necessary for the office and laboratories.

The single-storey flat-roofed restaurant also had an external double-wall facade, following the thermal wall philosophy of the western nave, and its roofscape contained dramatically formed air extracts. The materials were restricted to brown-coated steel sheeting on the main block, with bronze solar glazing to the new offices and restaurant. There was no mural, but the exposed steel columns in the glass link between the old and new buildings carried sharp spectrum colours, while the glazing graduated in colour from dark brown for the offices through sand and buff to clear in the laboratories.

The brown theme was extended to the entrance courtyard and enclosure walls where a hard, vitreous brown brick was employed. The inverted U-shaped entrance resembled a magnet, symbolising the induction forces that operated the intelligent pig being manufactured there, and incorporated a thin concrete slab projected to form a canopy. The complex was completed by a circular gatehouse, which oversaw a sunken car park. The land was liable to flooding, and by sinking the car park area a natural sump was created to deal with excess water on the site, and to thus protect the factory's precious equipment. Meanwhile, the success of the development and manufacture of the intelligent pig has ensured the building's survival in good order.

Notes

1 Wilfred Burns, *Newcastle: A Study in Replanning*, London, Leonard Hill, 1967, p44.

2 Malcolm McEwen, 'Prescription for Tyneside', *RIBA Journal*, vol. 72, no. 11, November 1965, p544.

3 Peter Yates, *Architects' Journal*, vol. 162, no. 46, 12 November 1975, p993.

4 F. J. Green, quoted in McEwen, op. cit.

5 Ryder and Yates, *Northern Architect*, no. 33, July 1966, p684.

6 Peter Yates, 'Architects' approach to Architecture', lecture 4 November 1975, part quoted in *Architects' Journal*, 12 November 1975, p993.

7 *The Journal,* 21 September, 1967, p7

8 Ibid., p7

9 Peter Yates 'Architects' approach to Architecture', lecture, op. cit.

10 *Sunday Times*, 15 December 1968.

West Hartlepool from Durham, Peter Yates, c.1958

CHAPTER EIGHT:
The Commercial World

Ryder and Yates's first major commission in the commercial world came, unusually, from the motor trade. However, the successful refurbishment of two garages, in Newcastle and Morpeth,[1] made them an obvious choice for R. H. Patterson's new Ford garage and showroom in Scotswood Road, Newcastle, built in 1962–4. The building was planned on two levels to take advantage of the steeply sloping site, thereby allowing an uncluttered showroom to oversail workshops placed underneath. The local planning authority insisted on a two-storey frontage to the Scotswood Road elevation, which this structural arrangement allowed.

The entire frontage of 60 metres was carried on three columns, providing maximum flexibility in the use of the floor space and an uninterrupted glass wall to the car showroom. The upper main structure was interesting in that it consisted of a steel space frame, a relatively new technology in Britain, first explored extensively in the North East. A tapered box was clad on top, with a ceiling beneath, and was supported by stanchions in the office walls. Steel beams carried the flat roof of the central office core and castella beams spanned the north bay, supported in the centre of the building by lattice girders. Above the showroom, these girders were set back from the glass face, while the roof trusses were inclined to impart a larger scale to the street elevation and to include huge advertising banners in the great depth of the roof.

The expression of the structure extended to the gables, whose profile followed the tapering shape of the roof trusses. Such an innovative structure owed much to the Polish engineer Leszek Kubik, of Mellows and Kubik, who in 1963 joined Ryder and Yates and brought his imaginative approach to structure to all their later buildings.

The Scotswood Road area of Newcastle, then dominated by the factories of Vickers Armstrong, was a new one for the motor trade, and customers had to be made aware of the location. The brief for Patterson's called for a building of striking appearance that would advertise the client. This was duly provided, not only by the flag panels in the main facade, but also by a chimney flue at the front of the showroom clad on all four sides by the Ford logo. This proved so successful that the client used it in an advertising slogan, 'Under the Big Ford Sign'.

The extended entrance lobby, the only projection on a flat facade, was also covered in the Ford logo printed on Formica panels, in varying sizes and fonts. The blank south elevation presented the company name and colour, in storey-high letters, to the passengers on the adjacent railway lines.

Patterson's garage,
Scotswood Road,
Newcastle

Patterson's garage:
plan of lower-floor
workshop

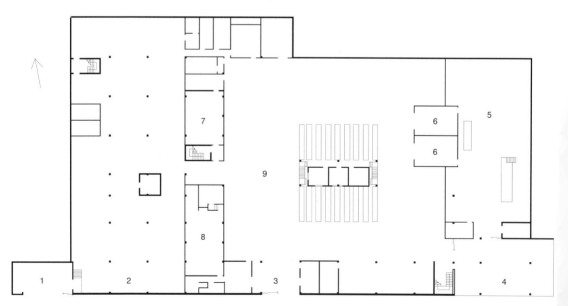

1	Loading Bay	6	Spray Booths
2	Parts Store	7	Canteen
3	Main Entrance	8	Office
4	Covered Entrance	9	Main Workshop
5	Body Shop		

Peter Yates's expertise in exhibition design was also used to great effect internally, where he used the logos from the range of Ford cars in a highly dramatic mural across the whole back wall of the showroom. The intention was to provide Patterson's with walls that did their publicity for them, making posters and other advertising material unnecessary.

Corporate colour limited the mural to black, grey and white, and allowed the widely varying lettering to form a lively background without distracting from the brightly coloured cars. By using mirrors and some inverted text, the length of the mural was apparently doubled. Although the building survives as a busy Ford dealership, under the original owners, the whole complex – including the service towers – has been over-clad in modular aluminium panels, including the first-floor banner recesses. Yates's graphics, signing and murals have also been destroyed.

The design for an exhibition stand for British Gypsum in 1962 had a second life when its steel frame was reused for Ryder and Yates's own offices, then being designed at Killingworth. The stand had resembled a small two-storey building, with its white facade, ribbon windows, flat roof and slender columns, and it was a relatively straight-forward task to design an office around the recycled steelwork. The new office was single-storey and rectilinear, with a continuous ribbon of glazing along each side extended to full height at the ends, within a frame of Formica panels. Inside, only the cloakrooms and lavatories were fully enclosed, the conference and interview rooms being divided by clear plate glass.

The result was an open-plan office where up to 40 architects and engineers could be housed in one space, an important demonstration of Ryder and Yates's

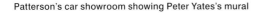
Patterson's car showroom showing Peter Yates's mural

The Ryder and Yates office

Ryder and Yates office layout

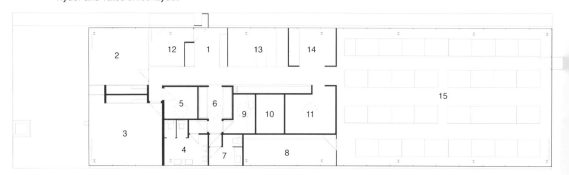

1	Entrance	9	Galley
2	Conference Room 1	10	Cleaner
3	Conference Room 2	11	Print Room
4	Male Bathroom	12	Reception
5	Interview Room	13	Secretaries
6	Cloaks	14	Models
7	Female Bathroom	15	Drawing Office
8	Library		

multi-disciplinary approach to building design. The building is unique among Ryder and Yates's office buildings in deliberately *not* being designed for expansion, as the partners firmly believed in retaining a modest size, with themselves firmly in control of all work within the office.

The sophisticated structural system consisted of elegant perimeter steel columns with lattice girders, which could span the office space without the need for intermediate support. Formica-faced timber panels and aluminium glazing were hung on the outside of the expressed columns to form the envelope for the new building. These were replaced with quartz-faced concrete panels in the 1970s, similar to those being developed by the practice at the time for their building for Sterling Organics. Ryder, the successors to Ryder and Yates, vacated the office in 2002. It is now leased by a computer services company and remains in good condition.

A factory unit for Lion Brushworks at Killingworth was designed in 1964 to provide 2,180 square metres of accommodation, including offices, a canteen, workshop, plating area and machine room. The unit, on a site opposite Ryder and Yates's own offices, had a brick superstructure, as it was related to standard industrial units rather than tailor-made to its process, while the workshop facade was clad in metal sheeting capable of extension. The main elevation was all of brick, with clerestory lighting, and given added visual interest by projecting display windows at ground-floor level. The office accommodation was enclosed within the main volume, making use of the height requirement for the factory but given two floors.

Lion Brushworks: south elevation

Lion Brushworks:
west elevation

The basic structure of the factory unit comprised steel portal frames of tapered castellated beam rafters at 7 metres. The tapered castells were designed to deal with the maximum structural movement at the centre, but were inclined to provide a fall to the roof deck. The inverted-V north lights were built up on the primary structure of tapered X-section cantilevers, with patent glazing to the north face. The glazing bars were designed as part of the roof light structure and did not affect the glazing. The last frame on the eastern facade was designed to accommodate future expansion, as was typical of Ryder and Yates's commercial buildings.

Artwork was given new scope here. Tension was given to the ordinary brickwork of the entrance elevation by a white stabilising channel that incorporated an 'alarm bell sliding on it like a scale rule'. To complement this, the external fuel tank in the car park entrance was given a sculptural role by being elevated up on a single support out of its shallow concrete basin. 'The oil tank, an acrobatic cube, hops on one foot and doubles as a trademark,' Yates explained.[2]

The building is no longer in use by Lion Brushworks and, although it is currently partly occupied, it is for sale.

The Citadel building,
Amberley at Killingworth

The two high-rise office blocks forming the Amberley Building were built in 1967 for Northumberland County Council, and formed the first part of the Citadel, as the town centre of the new Killingworth Township was known. This was a complex of shops, offices, public buildings and flats within a single megastructure, a little like the better-known example at Cumbernauld but with pedestrian walkways across the complex more closely related to the surrounding landscape.

Six floors of offices were raised 9 metres above the pedestrian deck, which served the shopping area of the town centre, and was linked via a pedestrian bridge to adjacent public housing. The structure was a composite system of steel and concrete with a flat glass facade, the use of air conditioning negating the need for opening windows. The colour of the St Gobain window glass was carefully matched to the brown aluminium enamelled spandrel panels to present a single face rather than the individual panel arrangement at Norgas House.

At ground level, the 15-metre-high columns, finished in black and split by a central rainwater pipe, were extended through the podium to the second floor. A feature was a concealed boiler house which was denoted externally only by a composition of earth

Two office blocks of Amberley – the first phase of the Citadel

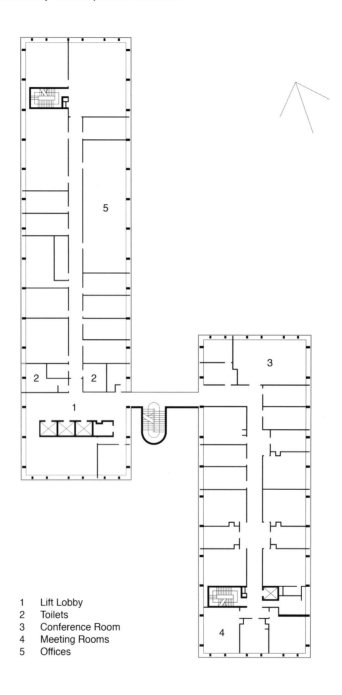

1   Lift Lobby
2   Toilets
3   Conference Room
4   Meeting Rooms
5   Offices

sculpture, three white chimneys and two rectilinear 'conning towers'. Amberley was demolished in the late 1990s.

In 1957, Tyne Tees Television began broadcasting for the new independent network from a former Egyptian cotton warehouse in City Road, Newcastle. A new communications tower was conceived as a column of light and, dominating the skyline, it became a symbol of the expanding company. It was required to allow disc relay aerials to be mounted at a height of 50 m from the ground, ensuring clearance above all local obstacles.

The converted buildings could not readily accommodate the additional loading of a tower, and it had to be carefully engineered. The solution adopted was an all-welded virendeel parallel box square cantilever 27 metres high, with sides 2 metres wide supported on a splayed angle base. As tension bracing was not necessary on this type of structure, access ladders and triangular landings were disposed along the diagonals of the tower box structure. The spinal trunking for continuous fluorescent lighting was secured to these stair flights, while the vertical cladding of light aluminium tees acted as an illuminated envelope and safety grid.

This unusual system was a direct result of Leszek Kubik's fascination with virendeel trusses after their successful use at the Engineering Research Station, and the circular

Amberley: flues and entrance to the subterranean boiler house

Photomontage of TTTV control tower by Peter Yates showing Tyneside landmarks

Sterling Organics entrance canopy, a variation of the ERS pylon

open-framed tower was in the best Ryder and Yates tradition, showing most clearly the close relationship between architect and engineer. A communications tower was also built for Northern Gas adjacent to Norgas House in Killingworth. Again a virendeel girder was utilised, although this one adopted a triangular form rather than the cylinder used for the television tower.

The commercial buildings of the 1970s continued Ryder and Yates's design vocabulary, with added confidence following the success of their earlier buildings. New technologies, materials and techniques unavailable in the 1960s were employed, adding an extra sophistication to what were still distinctively Ryder and Yates designs. Pharmaceutical companies joined existing clients in widening the architects' range of operations.

The 1972 brief from the pharmaceutical company Sterling Organics, based at Dudley, Northumberland, called for a main entrance, administrative offices and a restaurant, all to be capable of expansion. The location was within the firm's existing industrial complex which fronted a main road and faced terraces of small houses. The local planners were anxious that the environment of these houses should be improved by screening the older buildings housing the production processes. The new development comprised three buildings, linked by covered ways. Landscaping included a

Sterling Organics site layout

1	Entrance Lobby	6	Entrance
2	Kitchen	7	Boardroom
3	Restaurant	8	Reception
4	Pool	9	Director
5	Garden	10	Open Plan Office

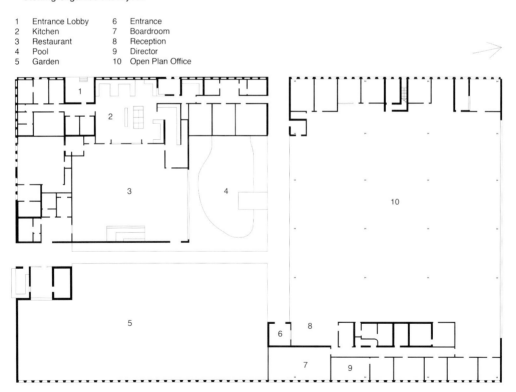

courtyard garden behind a facade wall placed to front any extension to the offices. A plant room above the offices was expressed by stylised extract flues.

The external walls were clad in modular pre-cast concrete panels to create a similar effect to that at the ERS, in that several activities, here in separate buildings, were regularised by a common style of facade. They were identically formed using exposed white quartz aggregate, and each had a single bull's eye window glazed directly into it, together with a vertical tear duct incised from sill to ground to allow water to run off. (A similar quartz finish was used when, in 1974, Ryder and Yates reclad their own offices.) More fully glazed panels enclosing an internal garden were painted internally in varying shades of green to echo the topiary effect of the landscape. Linear expansion could occur along this wall or out from the metal clad north elevation.

Within the entrance court, the facade of the main open-plan office was all glass, with structural glass ribs, while in the directors' office suites Pittsburgh solar reflective glass was used. The office reception area was clad in brick and top-lit by a parabolic roof light, as seen in many of the earlier houses. Another was found in the interview room but was formed of mirror glass with spotlighting behind to create an unusual illuminated effect. The parabolic section of the roof over the reception area containing these windows was spatially separated from the supporting walls.

Ryder and Yates used a number of devices to highlight entrances within the regular and uniform facades of their buildings, most famously the bridge and ceremonial arch at the entrance to the ERS. At Sterling Organics, again with a regular facade, they created a soaring cantilevered canopy, this time with a slender open pylon set almost horizontally and stretched to its structural limits. Artwork consisted of a Yates mural depicting the molecular structure of the firm's leading pharmaceutical product, paracetamol. This was enclosed within the mirror glazing to the conference room off the reception, where lighting behind the mirror repeated the pattern. All spaces were air-conditioned, and the handling plant was expressed, inevitably, as a sculptural form on the roof of the offices.

By the late 1970s even the most committed architects were aware that modernism was popularly perceived to have failed, and that a return to historical styles, whether neo-vernacular or post-modern classicism, seemed inevitable in Britain. The economic decline that the country experienced towards the end of the decade also affected architects and led many to re-examine their design philosophies to go with the fundamental changes in society as the welfare state was taken apart by Margaret Thatcher.

Although it was clear that modern architecture had had too ambitious a sense of its own power in thinking it could solve society's problems, Ryder and Yates did not abandon their beliefs. However, their buildings of the 1980s were fewer in number, while Yates's ill-health meant his influence was reduced, and he died in 1982. Structural engineering partner Leszek Kubik's search for innovative structural solutions was also lost, as he moved into academia. But the practice moved on to develop new architectural devices based on curtain walling and solutions to energy conservation.

Later buildings for Tyne Tees Television, beginning with Studio 5, were totally new

TTTV Studio 5 canopied entrance

buildings, unlike the earlier commission. The introduction of Channel Four to the independent television network meant that new production space was necessary, not only to relieve pressure on existing facilities but also to allow for future replacement and upgrading. Studio 5 and its associated car park were the first new buildings in the Tyne Tees complex, located on a steeply sloping site with a public house, the Egypt Cottage, set between them and the existing buildings.

The location of the pub and its associated rights of light, determined the position of the studio set back from the street, and thereby gave Ryder and Yates a perfect justification for a canopied entrance, here covered by a glazed barrel vault. At the end of the arcade, a break between it and the entrance doors heralded a symbolic, stylised version of the Minoan horns used on Norgas House.

These rectilinear concrete forms were a skeletal reversed version of the earlier model, perhaps more symbolic of an over-sized tuning fork, which was perhaps appro-

TTTV studio 5 exterior

The Vickers factory on the banks of the Tyne

priate considering Tyne Tees's role in the vanguard of popular music broadcasting in the early 1980s with *The Tube* – named after the entrance walkway. The actual entrance was formed from a glass cube, another favourite device of Ryder and Yates, with white columns offering support. The foyer housed a reception desk similar to the furniture found in Norgas House and ERS.

A building contemporary with Studio 5 was Terry Farrell's complex for TV-am in London. Both buildings were in run-down areas and owed little to their surroundings, but while one was an exercise in fashionable post-modernism, the other remained coolly modern. However, the future of the TTTV building is uncertain, as the company has vacated the site.

A tank factory for Vickers Armaments at Scotswood, completed in 1981, replaced a series of existing works scattered over several miles in the west of the city between the Tyne and Scotswood Road. They included the original Elswick works established by William Armstrong, the 19th-century armaments manufacturer. Ryder and Yates's new design used simple portal frames, with roof purlins and aluminium cladding sheets designed to span 2 metres.

They adopted a standard developer's package that had used computers to design structural components to the smallest, and therefore most economical, size possible. Using these parameters, a building was created almost half a kilometre long and consisting of a central main bay of 25 metres span with two side bays of 15 metres each. To house ancillary accommodation on the north facade, the cross section was extended by a further 6 metres, and for the offices on the south side the section was increased by 30 metres.

The simple structural solution of increasing the cross section where necessary from the standard three bays that ran the full length of the building offered great economies to the client, and this made the project financially viable. The height of the main nave of the building was determined by that of the equipment to be housed. Because of old

Vickers riverside entrance

machine bays, services and railway lines across the site, with poor sub-soil and the foundations of earlier buildings, a system of continuous wide concrete strips supported the portal frames and reduced the load of the building, while avoiding the excessive cutting-out of existing bases. The reuse of Vickers' original machinery with a new system of founding proved very economical. These machines could move but not distort, so they were floated on the ground on concrete rafts, a radical departure for the support of heavy industrial machinery, which hitherto had always been solidly fixed.

Because of its sheer scale and problems of economic constraints, the Vickers factory demanded a special cladding. Research on an adjacent factory for Michell Bearings had shown that fibre cement sheet was the cheapest and most suitable. However, as its armaments factory was so prestigious, Vickers eventually opted for more expensive, but more easily maintained, silver aluminium sheeting, but its use had to be carefully controlled. It relied for its impact on a minimum of simple yet powerful effects.

The long building had no apparent change of scale or form on the main facade other than a restless yellow gutter that ran up and down to signal entrances or enclosures and reached its climax over the entrance in the form of an inverted V. The aluminium was used only above the gutter on the north (road) side of the building, but was extended to the ground on the south (river) side, where a complementary aesthetic took over for the offices in a projecting extension set under a natural continuation of the roof slope. There, a perforated concrete screen signalled the entrance to the offices, a device which appeared earlier in a more abstract form in the stand for British Gypsum and in the Amberley offices.

To achieve the relatively high insulation requirements of industrial buildings, foam insulation was used in conjunction with the aluminium sheeting. An airtight structure was achieved by a combination of curved eaves and oval-shaped windows (with neoprene gaskets) that suited the corrugations in the cladding.

Because of the minimum airflow required for welding and plating, it was possible to use direct-fired gas heaters, with no flue, while roof fans provided ventilation and gave direct down draught in summer and recirculated air in winter. Although Vickers was sold to Alvis, who were in turn taken over by British Aero Systems, the building still functions in its original role of manufacturing tanks, and is in good order.

Notes

1   Fox and Hounds Garage, West Road, Newcastle, 1961, and Adams and Gibbons Garage, Morpeth.
2   Peter Yates, *Northern Perspective*, vol. 2, no. 1, March–April 1972, pp8–9; 'Architects' approach to architecture', lecture November 1975, part quoted in *Architects' Journal*, vol. 162, no. 46, 12 November 1975, p993.

Polperro, Cornwall, Peter Yates, c. 1956

CHAPTER NINE:
Building for the Community

During the 1960s Ryder and Yates produced a series of buildings for healthcare and welfare. Like Tecton before them, they wanted to demonstrate the way in which modern architecture could serve society, and their buildings continue the tradition of the Finsbury Health Centre of 1938 and Le Corbusier's Cité de Refuge in Paris of 1931–3 for the Armé du Salut. Ryder and Yates similarly built for the Salvation Army, as well as the local health authority and local government. The Finsbury Health Centre was one of the last major designs by Lubetkin and Tecton, and the building had a significant effect on Ryder and Yates's approach to architecture, with its bridge access, mix of permanent and flexible planning elements, the parabolic form of its penthouse structure and mural by Gordon Cullen.

The first welfare commission for Ryder and Yates came from the local health authority, with two baby clinics in Newcastle in 1960. Both were sited within large housing estates, at Fawdon in the north of the city and at Fenham in the west. They established the practice's reputation for buildings of real social value. The clinics followed a similar format, with medical facilities at ground level and two flats for midwives or policemen above. They were organised around a large central waiting area, with consulting rooms, examination and therapy areas, and toilets all accessed from this space.

Ryder's planning philosophy of minimum circulation and corridor areas was put to the test to realise such a brief on a domestic scale. The clinics were flat roofed and built of brick, with a glazed facade to the waiting area and a band of clerestory glazing effectively separating the two floors. Circular white columns, a device used in many of the earlier houses, carried the first floor. As the area of the clinic exceeded that necessary for the two flats, the rear ground-floor ancillary spaces were decked to provide a private balcony. Concrete barrel-vaulted canopies signified the entrances on the main facade, semicircular in profile at Fawdon and parabolic at Fenham. Fenham has been extensively remodelled by the addition of a pitched roof and reorganised fenestration, while the clinic at Fawdon has been demolished.

The first of a series of projects for the Salvation Army was the Hopedene Maternity Home, built in Elswick Road in 1969 as an extension to a large Victorian house. It replaced an earlier labour ward with a new wing for six mothers. It was designed as the first part of a major development, which envisaged the replacement of the Victorian mansion, Hopedene, and the addition of a second storey. Meanwhile, the architects had

Ryder and Yates

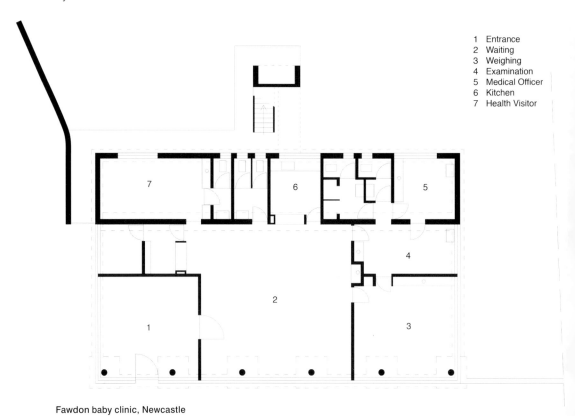

1 Entrance
2 Waiting
3 Weighing
4 Examination
5 Medical Officer
6 Kitchen
7 Health Visitor

Fawdon baby clinic, Newcastle

Hopedene Maternity Home

Hopedene Maternity Home: west elevation of the maternity wing

to relate to the older building, and fill a gap in the street between it and another house belonging to the Salvation Army, concealing the garden behind. The simple linear plan adopted belied the complex structure necessary to accommodate changes in level and provision for its extension.

The dramatic solution of cantilevering the new wing over the steeply sloping site was accentuated by using darker brickwork for the upper floor. The lower floor, which housed ancillary spaces, followed the steep gradient of the site and was clad in a lighter brick and set back to allow the main floor to be dominant. The wards overlooked the large west-facing garden, while the eastern elevation was opened up with only a minimum number of slit windows to achieve the privacy and quiet essential in a home for young mothers. Its brindle brick was chosen for ease of matching should the building be extended. But after a review of its role in the care of young women, the Salvation Army handed over the building to the local authority social services, and it was demolished in the 1990s.

The Men's Social Services Centre for the Salvation Army, adjoining Tyne Tees Television's studios in City Road and completed in 1974, replaced a 'Men's Palace' or itinerants' hostel that had been demolished for an office development. The new hostel, a curved linear building in blue brindle brick, sat in a commanding position alongside the 17th-century Keelman's Hospital in Newcastle's City Road.

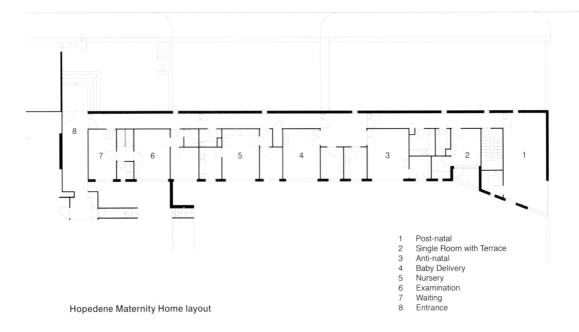

Hopedene Maternity Home layout

1 Post-natal
2 Single Room with Terrace
3 Anti-natal
4 Baby Delivery
5 Nursery
6 Examination
7 Waiting
8 Entrance

Men's Palace, Newcastle: south elevation to City Road

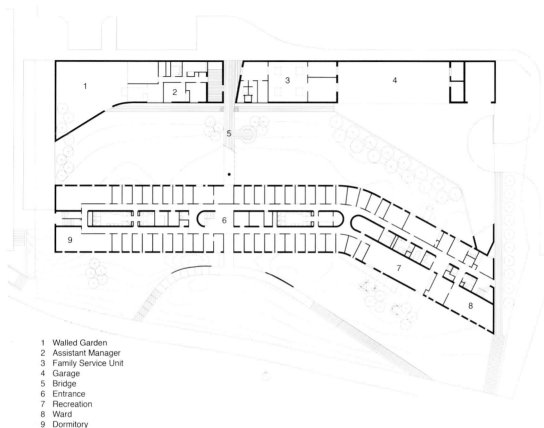

1 Walled Garden
2 Assistant Manager
3 Family Service Unit
4 Garage
5 Bridge
6 Entrance
7 Recreation
8 Ward
9 Dormitory

Men's Palace layout

Ryder first proposed two parallel blocks, but then noted a proposed road improvement plan that introduced a curve – which prompted him to change the roadside block. This three-storey range held the principal accommodation, with bedrooms on the ground and second floors and communal rooms on the first. It housed 184 men in dormitories and small rooms, and there were day rooms, a restaurant, facilities for the elderly and a small hospital.

The carefully arranged fenestration, its proportions echoing those of Le Corbusier's Modular, allowed for maximum flexibility in the plan so that three bedroom units could be formed from two if required, while having an asymmetry that played down the building's institutional aspect. This apparently casual arrangement of windows was interrupted at first-floor level by a glass oriel window to the dining room. A curved access ramp to the central entrance was set under a boomerang-shaped canopy redolent of that at Highpoint II, especially in its asymmetry, but instead of caryatids it was supported on thin tubular steel columns. The path to it, along the front of the building, was punctuated by one of Peter Yates's familiar earth sculptures.

Men's Palace: ceremonial link between blocks (opposite)

Social Services Centre: internal courtyard terrace and garden (below)

MEA House, Newcastle

MEA House competition drawing

The rear access to the north was via the equally familiar propylaeum and ceremonial bridge. Staff quarters at roof level completed the composition, with another penthouse of parabolic section.

The nature of the building suggested the use of hard, uncompromising materials that would require little maintenance and be hygienic. Blue brindle brickwork was commonly used by the practice as exterior cladding, and was here also used internally. The full height narrow strip windows were formed from steel, pivoted vertically, and had bright green sliding shutters to give unity to the facade that other curtain devices could not provide. The building continues to function as a social services centre for the Salvation Army.

While the Newcastle Social Services Centre broadly followed the traditional plan of a Men's Palace, the design for a centre in Sunderland, made in 1982, adopted a more radical concept. The Sunderland centre was to be a true social centre to benefit the community at large, not only the homeless. It was to reflect the Salvation Army's new role of providing accommodation for a number of semi-independent groups, supervised in accordance with their particular needs, including women at risk, alcoholics and recidivists.

The centre replaced a Men's Palace just outside the city centre, on a site near the docks and enclosed by existing developments on three sides and a busy road to the other. The resulting H-plan with a courtyard was particularly redolent of Finsbury Health Centre, with a central core containing the entrance and communal facilities flanked by two wings of accommodation. A ceremonial entrance under a cantilevered concrete canopy, complete with an illuminated sign, enhanced the comparison.

The Social Services Centre in Sunderland was in many ways the antithesis of the Men's Palace in Newcastle, in that the design was introspective. Here the perimeter of the building followed the line of the street, with no room for external landscaping. The building could be appreciated, in a metaphysical sense, as a castle – because its high walls, coming straight out of the street and punctuated only by a few small windows to a regular pattern, suggested total security from a hostile society.

This metaphor was completed with the cantilevered access bridge offering a form of 'drawbridge'. As the visitors and tenants walked up the ramp they could be easily monitored from the residents' lounge and a reception office with an oval window. The brick and tile aesthetic used at Newcastle was repeated in the Sunderland centre, where the two wings were formed from blue brindle brick, and the central core was faced in matching tiles and set back from the main facade to reduce its bulk.

Ryder and Yates's first major building of real urban scale in the centre of Newcastle followed a limited competition. Three benefactors, Mungo Campbell, Esther McCracken and Alastair Fife, offered to provide a building for several charitable organisations to be housed together. The resulting community services building in Ellison Place, known as MEA House from the initials of its begetters and built in 1974, was designed to complete a square formed by Rutherford College (now Northumbria University), the Church of Divine Unity and the YMCA.

The competition brief requested that it relate to the college in floor levels and overall height, and that the existing road pattern around the square be maintained. The height limitation, pedestrian access provision and restricted floor plate meant that every available portion of space had to be used effectively. Moreover, the building had to relate to a proposed motorway that was due to be built to the west, and to incorporate a pedestrian ramp and bridge leading to the city centre.

Ryder and Yates won the competition for their original solution of lifting the main two-storey accommodation block up two floors to allow access to the square, and to incorporate an auditorium. One entrance at ground level from the square gave direct access to the hall and services, while vertical circulation cores, containing stairs, lifts and services, extended through all four floors. The auditorium on the ground floor stood outside the rectilinear main block and followed the curved outline of the site in a relationship similar to that of the foyer and office block at Norgas House.

There was again also a penthouse with a parabolic roof. The structural system necessary to realise this solution was unique, however. The three circulation cores supported virendeel trusses at roof level, which in turn carried outrigger frames with hangers to carry the floor beams and external cladding. The suspended floors were formed of concrete slabs carried on cantilevered steel beams, and the girders were braced at main roof level and expressed internally in the penthouse roof. Trusses and frames carried curved, inverted T-supports for the penthouse to receive a metal deck, with the main roof being carried on the struts of the outrigger frame.

The structural solution was expressed clearly on the gable walls, the profile of the cross section exactly echoing the nature of the suspension structure. The parabolic outline of the penthouse and the exposed diagonal hangers, with the vertical sides and base deeply indented, provided an accurate expression of the supporting service towers and contained the pedestrian deck. The cores to the north and south contained stairs and had wing halls cantilevered out to meet the cladding, while the central core contained lifts, services and toilets. At ground level, the independent curved auditorium was formed of post-tensioned brickwork. The air handling system discharged at window level, which, together with the lighting system, was arranged to suit the requirements of a flexible partitioning system.

The main elevations, facing east onto the square and west towards the intended motorway, were clad in Corning mirror glass set in aluminium frames. The use of this glass, imported from Pittsburgh, with its soft quality that distorted reflections, was inspired by a trip made by Ryder and Yates to the Montreal Expo, where it was featured on one of the pavilions. For Yates it was 'a magic mirror on the wall. Our facades no longer embody a fixed and arbitrary choice of pattern and texture, but are instead a literal reflection of the place itself. It is good manners and architecture taken to the limit.'[1]

The concrete gabled end walls were faced in a glass aggregate resin finish, struck to resemble fixed panels. Smooth brown brindle brick was used throughout the ground floor, inside and out, with aluminium faced roofing felt to both the main and penthouse

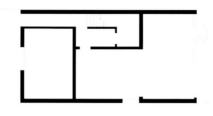

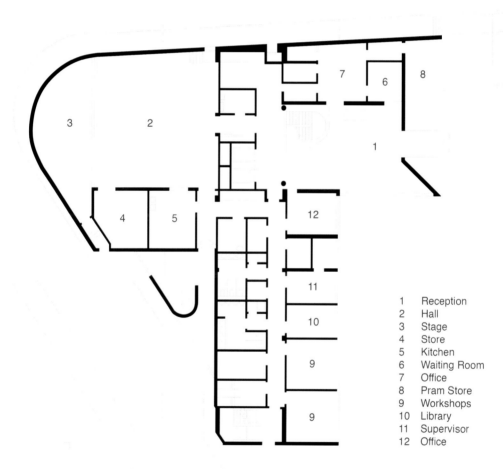

1 Reception
2 Hall
3 Stage
4 Store
5 Kitchen
6 Waiting Room
7 Office
8 Pram Store
9 Workshops
10 Library
11 Supervisor
12 Office

MEA House layout

MEA House, Newcastle

roofs. The high cost of bridging the access road, together with that of the structure and external finishes, meant the internal finishes were very simple, with PVC tiled floors, painted plaster walls and acoustic tiled suspended ceilings.

The extraordinary constraints inflicted on the designers may in fact have inspired Ryder and Yates to produce one of Newcastle's finest modern buildings. The motorway was never built and the adjacent terraces were not demolished, but MEA House sits well next to them – it is one of the centre's best pieces of townscape, and the first offices in the country designed for a range of voluntary services. MEA House was refurbished by Ryders in 2000 and still functions as a community services building. As Stephen Gardiner wrote in 1976:

The Ryder and Yates design transcends detail: the architects have used their building to turn Ellison Place into a square, the detail has to fit this conception, which is how it should be. But to make a building that closes the corners of the square (unlike the YMCA) means a structure that will bridge the road, and it is this bridge construction of cantilevered floor from a central structure, which leads naturally to the airy glass facade that mirrors sky and clouds.

MEA House is so sharp and shiny, so powerful and bright, that it assumes complete command of the square, and becomes the focus of it. The other buildings withdraw like embarrassed shadows. A real competition winner.[2]

Notes

1   Peter Yates, 'Architects' approach to architecture', *Architects' Journal*, vol. 162, no. 46, 12 November 1975, p993.
2   Stephen Gardiner, *Observer*, 1976.

Oia, Santorini, Greece by Peter Yates, date unknown

Epilogue

In declining health, Peter Yates undertook a trip to Greece, filling sketchbooks which would form the basis of paintings and models on his return to Newcastle.[1] His death from cancer on 16 November 1982 at the age of only 62 robbed the practice of his influence as form maker, and severed the direct link with Le Corbusier. Not long afterwards, Berthold Lubetkin wrote:

> Some years ago I was talking with Le Corbusier about Peter Yates, with whose work he was familiar. 'This boy can see things,' said he, but to me it seemed more relevant that Peter could do things.

> *In his paintings he prodded the depths rather than depicting the surface.*
> *Simmering passions behind the stony immobility.*
> *Cathedrals like rocks and rocks like cathedrals. From the vision*
> *of his beloved Durham locked in the midst of time to the*
> *Ultramarine rhapsody of Cyclopic islands.*
> *By staking claims on the distance he excites the imagination.*
> *Simplicity, directness and purity give his work the power.*
> *That was Peter Yates my friend the poet architect.*
> *The song is over but the chords go on vibrating.*[2]

In 1981, Gordon Ryder, in an article in the *Architects' Journal*, wrote of his disappointment with modern architecture, and the attacks made on it led by the Prince of Wales.

> We are in a period where a certainty of direction is unsure. The blossoming of the Modern Movement from the beginning of the century when its basic philosophy of an architecture reflecting its position in a machine age and largely bereft of its craft base became widely accepted. It has now become widely misunderstood.

> Its apparent simplicity of design has itself been responsible for the production of countless artless buildings. The response to this, partly assisted by royal decree, has been a return to the imitation of other periods, a direction that will lead to lifeless buildings in spite of the incorporation of details from works of eternal beauty.

Architectural design must return and extend from its roots created by such designers, from Corbusier and to the present day works of Foster and Rogers. The need for decoration will be satisfied by artist architects and not by the application of art to buildings.[3]

After Yates's death, Ted Nicklin, already an associate partner, was elevated to full status and the practice renamed the Ryder Nicklin Partnership. A clause in their agreement decreed that the partners must retire at 70, so Gordon had to go in 1989, with Ted elected as heir apparent. Tragically that was to prove short-lived as Ted died in 1994. A younger partner, Peter Buchan, took over to build the firm into what it is today. Gordon Ryder died in 2000.

Ryder and Yates made a unique contribution to the architecture of the North East. Perhaps when more people are made aware of this, more care might be given their surviving works.

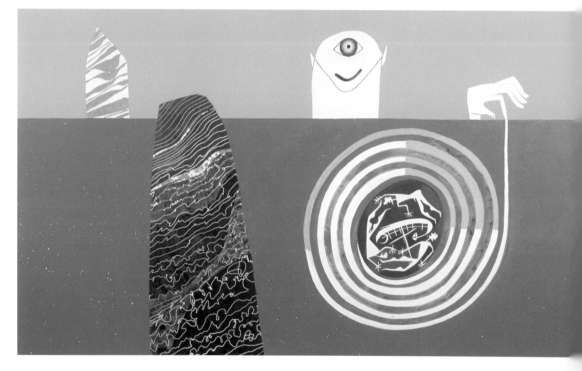

Cyclops Rock, Greece, Peter Yates, c.1978

Notes

1   Interview with Adam Yates.
2   Written by Berthold Lubetkin in 1985 and given to the author by Jolyon Yates, Peter's son.
3   Gordon Ryder, *Architects' Journal*, vol. 173, no. 4, 28 January 1981, p148.

List of Works

Introduction

The following list provides a guide to all the buildings and projects undertaken by Ryder and Yates. The list of works has been arranged chronologically and includes selected published references, awards, journals, competitions and unexecuted projects.

Key

 Award

 Journal reference

 Competition

 Unexecuted project

A double asterisk (**) indicates that the building has been demolished.
A single asterisk (*) indicates that it has been drastically altered, sometimes beyond recognition.
Minor alterations, such as changes of windows, are not noted although most of the buildings have suffered from this.

Chronological list of selected projects

c.1951

Clubhouse for Tynemouth Sailing Club
Priors Haven, Tynemouth
Client: Tynemouth Sailing Club

1952

Walker House
Woolsington Park, Northumberland
Client: Dr W. Walker

1952

Compressor house
Long Meg, Cumbria
Client: Carlisle Plaster Company

1953

 Beach houses
Unexecuted project
Beadnell, Northumberland
Client: A. Stanger and J. Johnstone

📖 *Evening Chronicle*, 1 September 1953, 'Beadnell Houses'

📖 *Architectural Design*, April 1954, 'Beadnell Houses'

1953

Exhibition stand**
Olympia, London
Client: Gotham Plaster Company

1954

Harlequin*
Gill Road, Scotby, Cumberland
Client: Derek Damerell

Built by J. T. Laing for £5,000

📖 *Architectural Review*, November 1956, pp325–7

📖 *Builder*, 23 May 1958, pp940–1

📖 *House and Garden*, May 1956, cover and feature on Damerell House

📖 *Newcastle Journal*, 17 September 1957, 'Modern Architects make best use of Modern Techniques', discussion of Damerell, Mamourian, Saint and Liddell Houses

1954

Hill House farmhouse*
Walton, Brampton, Northumberland
Client: M. Steven

1954–5

Offices at Gotham, Nottingham
Client: Gotham Plaster Company

1956

Black House*
52 Brierdene Crescent, Whitley Bay
Built by J. Hill

📖 *Evening Chronicle*, 12 August 1956, 'Whitley Bay Houses'

1956

Allan House
68 Brierdene Crescent, Whitley Bay
Built by J. Hill in conjunction with no. 52, although of a different design

📖 *Evening Chronicle*, 12 August 1956, 'Whitley Bay Houses'

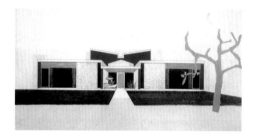

68 Brierdene Crescent, Whitley Bay

1956

Friar's Gate*
Hayton, Cumberland
Client: J. F. Tonner

📖 *Cumberland News*, 18 January 1960

✳ Civic Trust county amenity award

1956

🏛 **Carlisle Civic Centre**
Unexecuted project

🏆 Second premium

1957

Exhibition stand**
Olympia, London
Client: British Plaster and Boards
Company

1957

Oakley House*
South View, Hayton Town Head,
Carlisle, Cumberland
Client: Charles Oakley

📖 *Northern Architect*, March/April
1963, p.197, 'Post War Housing in
Cumberland', Damerell and Oakley
Houses

Status: Heavily remodelled

1957

Saint House and surgery*
Longbenton
Client: Dr T. M. S. Saint

Status: Surgery demolished

The Saint House and surgery, Newcastle,
view from the south

1958

Liddell House*
Grand Parade, Tynemouth
Client: J. M. Liddell

📖 *Newcastle Journal*, 17 September
1957, 'Modern Architects make best
use of Modern Techniques'

📖 *Daily Express*, 10 April 1958,
'Stunner', article on Liddell House

Status: Heavily remodelled

📖 *Architectural Review*, August 1956,
pp105–7

1959

Mamourian House
Stanton Hall, Near Morpeth
Client: Alice Mamourian

📖 *Northern Architect*, September/
October 1964, p396, 'Mamourian
House'

📖 *Sunday Sun*, 30 August 1959, 'The
ultra-modern house in the heart of the
country'

1959

Beacon House flats
Whitley Bay
Client: J. M. Liddell

📖 *Northern Architect*, November 1961,
'Beacon House, Whitley Bay'

1959

Exhibition stand**
Olympia, London
Client: British Plaster and Boards
Company

📖 *Northern Architect*, May 1959,
'Designing for the Exhibition'

📖 *The Builder*, 4 December 1959,
G. G. Baines, 'Olympus Revisited'

1960

Clubhouse for Beadnell Sailing Club
Harbour Road, Beadnell
Client: Beadnell Sailing Club

1960

House in Vane Hill, Torquay
Client: J.M. Liddell

1960

Bank refurbishment*
High Street Hexham
Client: Martins Bank (later Barclays Bank)

1960

Children's clinic**
Strathmore Road, Fawdon, Newcastle
Client: Newcastle Area Health Authority

1960

Children's clinic*
Fenham Hall Drive, Fenham
Client: Newcastle Area Health Authority

1960

Legislative Council Building
Unexecuted project
Kampala, Uganda

c.1960

Garage and car showroom*
Morpeth
Client: Fox and Hounds group

1961

Garage and car showroom**
West Road, Newcastle
Client: Fox and Hounds group

1962

Redbridge Tower
The Avenue, Southampton
Client: Dor Properties

Northern Architect, March 1962, p.46

1962

Banking hall and offices
High Street, Sunderland
Client: NCPBS (later Northern Rock)

✳ Civic Trust Award, 1966

1962

Opticians**
Pilgrim Street, Newcastle
Client: F. Robson and Co.

✳ Civic Trust Commendation 1963

Status: Original shop front demolished and replaced

1962

Banking hall and offices**
St Mary's Place, Newcastle
Client: NCPBS (later Northern Rock)

1963

Public housing*
St Cuthbert's Green, Fenham
Client: Newcastle Corporation

Pilot scheme for Kenton development

📖 *The Journal*, 7 September 1967,
'Good housing designs take top
awards', St Cuthbert's Green,
Fenham

✳ Civic Trust Commendation, 1966

✳ Good Design in Housing Medal 1966
Heavily remodelled, with the addition
of pitched roofs and new windows

1963

🏚 **Durham Law Courts and Offices
for the Water Authority**
Unexecuted project

1964

Exhibition stand**
Olympia, London
Client: British Gypsum Company
Recycled as ...

Carlite Plaster stand at Olympia, 1953

1964

Offices
Northumbrian Way, Killingworth
Client: Ryder and Yates

R&Y later replaced original Formica
faced plywood panels with exposed
aggregate concrete

Status: Now computer software
company offices

1964

Garage and showroom*
Scotswood Road, Newcastle
Client: R. H. Patterson main Ford
dealer

📖 *Northern Architect*, May 1965,
pp494–502

📖 *Builder*, 30 October 1964, pp923–4

1964

Banking hall and offices**
Market Street, Newcastle
Client: NCPBS (later Northern Rock)

1964

Factory and offices
Northumbrian Way, Killingworth
Client: Lion Brush Works

📖 *Northern Perspectives*, March/April
1972, pp8–9

📖 *Newcastle Journal*, 24 January 1973

📖 *Building*, 24 March 1972, pp36–7

📖 *Design*, June 1973, pp42–4

Status: Empty

1964

Offices and works
Northumbrian Way, Killingworth
Client: K&L Marine
Empty

1964

Housing
Kenton Bar, Newcastle
Client: Newcastle Corporation

1965

Headquarters Building*
Killingworth
Client: Northern Gas Board

📖 *Architectural Review*, April 1966,
pp256–61

📖 *Northern Architect*, July 1966,
pp680–90

✳ RIBA Architecture Award, 1966

✳ Concrete Society Commendation
1968

✳ Civic Trust Award, 1968

Status: Horns removed during 1990s
refurbishment

1967

House, Middle Drive, Woolsington
Client: J. G. Ryder

📖 *House and Garden*, February 1972,
pp46–9, 'How to cope with an airport
a mile away'

📖 *House and Garden*, Guide to Interior
Design and Decoration 1972–3
pp80–1

📖 *Daily Mail*, 1 April 1976, p30, article on
Ryder House

1967

Engineering Research Station,
Killingworth,
Client: British Gas Council
Listed grade II

📖 *Architects' Journal*, 24 April 1968,
'Engineering Research Station'

📖 *Northern Architect*, September 1968,
p102

✳ Financial Times Award for Industrial
Architecture, 1968

✳ Civic Trust Commendation, 1968

✳ RIBA Award, 1969

✳ Concrete Society Award, 1968

Status: Latterly offices for North
Tyneside Metropolitan Council, now
vacant

1967

Amberley Office Blocks**
Citadel, Killingworth
Client: Northumberland County
Council

📖 *Evening Chronicle*, 19 September
1966, 'Killingworth captures big City
firm'

📖 *Architect and Building News*, 17
September 1970, 'System of curtain
glazing'

Status: Demolished in late 1990s

1967

Koh-i-nor Restaurant
Bigg Market, Newcastle

1968

Communications Tower
City Road, Newcastle
Client: Tyne Tees Television

1968

🔲 Tyne Deck
Unexecuted project
Newcastle/Gateshead

📖 *Northern Architect*, May 1969,
pp69–73

📖 *The Journal*, December 1969

1968

🔲 Newcastle Playhouse
Unexecuted project

1969

Control Room and Studio 1
City Road, Newcastle
Client: Tyne Tees Television

Status: TTTV moved out 2005, now
vacant

Stephenson House, Killingworth

1969

Stephenson House
Offices, Killingworth
Client: Northern Gas Pension Fund

1969

Hopedene Maternity Home**
Newcastle
Client: The Salvation Army

📖 *Architects' Journal*, 26 May 1971

1970

Training Centre, Killingworth*
Client: Northern Gas

📖 *Architects' Journal*, 8 September
1971, pp510–1

📖 *Bauen & Wohnen*, August 1972,
pp364–6

📖 *Deutche Bauzeitung*, October 1973,

📖 *Architects' Journal*, May 1974

✳ Galvanizing Design Award, 1970

✳ Structural Steel Design Award:
Architects, 1971

✳ Structural Steel Award: Steelwork

✳ Financial Times Commendation, 1971

Status: Remodelled by computer
services company

1970

🔲 Pavli Library
Unexecuted project
Tehran, Iran

1970

MEA House, Newcastle

First premium, completed 1976

1972

Offices and laboratories
Dudley, Northumberland
Client: Sterling Organics

1974

Men's hostel, Newcastle
Client: The Salvation Army

1974

Computer centre
Norgas House, Killingworth
Client: Northern Gas

Architects' Journal, 19 February 1975

Building Design, 28 November 1975, p12. Financial Times Industrial Architectural Award to Norgas Computer Building

Financial Times Award, 1975

1974

Community services building
Ellison Place, Newcastle
Client: MEA Trust,

Architectural Review, December 1975, pp368–73

Northern Architect, April 1976

RIBA Journal, May 1970, pp213–5

Building, 6 March 1970, pp59–61

RIBA Commendation, 1976

Civic Trust Award, 1979

1974

School of Engineering,
Killingworth
Client: British Gas Council

RIBA Commendation, 1978

1974

Albany village housing*
Washington
Client: Washington Development Corporation

1975

Northampton County Hall
Unexecuted project

1976

Printing works and offices
Fawdon, Newcastle
Client: Tyneside Printers

1976

On-line Inspection Centre,
Cramlington
Client: British Gas

1976

Pellos Timber Processing Facility
Unexecuted project
Tyne Dock, South Shields

1978

Burrell Collection
Unexecuted project

1979

🖾 **Crown Estate Housing**
Unexecuted project
Milbank, London

1980

House, Triangles
Riding Mill, Northumberland
Client: J. G. Ryder

1980

🖾 **Kew Gardens**
Unexecuted project
London

📖 *Architects' Journal*, 1 September 1982
pp34–8

1981

Tyneside Armstrong Works
Newcastle upon Tyne
Client: Vickers Armaments

📖 *Building*, 14 May 1982, pp30–2

📖 *Architects' Journal*, September 1982

✳ Civic Trust Award, 1983

1981

Studio 5 and car park
Newcastle
Client: Tyne Tees Television

📖 *Architects' Journal*, 14 October 1981

Status: Now vacant

1981

Housing
Ryhope, Sunderland
Client: Sunderland Corporation

1982

Social services centre, Sunderland
Client: The Salvation Army

1982

Tank factory
Leeds
Client: Vickers Armaments

1982

Vickers Ltd, Gemini
Completed 1982

1983

ICI Pavilion, Stoneleigh

🏆 First premium, completed 1984

Vickers riverside entrance

Front cover of Le Corbusier exhibition catalogue, Peter Yates, 1976

Exhibitions

Ryder and Yates

Art, Machine and Environment
The Hatton Gallery, Newcastle upon Tyne

Architecture and You
1958 Laing Art Gallery, featuring Damerell House

Peter Yates

Ultramarinos, a Mediterranean Odyssey
1975, Colbert Gallery, Durham City

England!
1976 Colbert Gallery, Durham City

England 2
1978, Downstairs Gallery, Newcastle upon Tyne

Central Sea, paintings of the Mediterranean
1979, Downstairs Gallery, Newcastle

Paris!
1982, Pen Gallery, Blackheath, London

The Lakes
1982, Bridge House Gallery, Coniston

Peter Yates Retrospective
1982, Hatton Gallery, Newcastle upon Tyne

Peter Yates
1983, 26 March – 17 April, DLI Museum and Arts Centre, Durham City

Peter Yates
1985, RIBA Gallery, London

Other Exhibitions

Le Corbusier Lithographs
Curated by Peter Yates
Ferens Art Gallery, Hull, 1976

Obituary – Gordon Ryder

J. Gordon Ryder Dip TP RIBA OBE, 5 December 1919 to 1 December 2000

The precision-designed architectural sculpture of the Engineering Research Station at Killingworth is a fitting memorial to the creative vision of Gordon Ryder, who died last month. The practice of Ryder and Yates pioneered and dominated the development of modern architecture in the North of England from the early 1960s, where their uncompromising approach to modernism distinguished them from their contemporaries.

Born in 1919, Gordon Ryder read architecture at Kings College, Durham University, qualifying in the same year as his close friend Peter Smithson. In 1948, he joined Berthold Lubetkin who had been appointed architect/planner for Peterlee New Town in County Durham, and it was here that he met his future partner, Peter Yates. For Lubetkin and his team, the next two years were to be stifled with post-war bureaucracy and resistance to the ideal of the creation of a progressive and humane architecture. In 1950, having exercised a quality of imagination and principled judgements that they were not prepared to compromise further, Lubetkin and his whole team resigned. Lubetkin left architectural practice altogether, Gordon Ryder set up his own practice, and Yates moved to Paris.

In 1953, the Ryder and Yates Partnership was formed, concentrating initially on private houses, exhibition stand designs and shop fronts. Their first major commission was for a Ford dealer's showroom (1964), for which there had been no precedent. In this building, the entire complex frontage of 70 metres was carried on three columns, allowing an uninterrupted glass showroom wall of 40 metres. The extraordinary use of space, structure and materials, colour arrangement and graphics demonstrated the architect's skill and control, producing a beautiful yet simple building.

It rapidly became obvious to Ryder that the only way to design buildings was not to design them as architects normally did – on their own – but in conjunction with other people who were very much part of the design operation. This led to the formation of a multi-disciplinary practice of architects and engineers, which allowed their philosophy of organisational flexibility to express itself in their philosophy of design.

The success of this approach was demonstrated most convincingly in their design for the Northern Gas Board offices, Norgas House, which commenced in April 1963 and was completed in March 1965. Norgas House was the first major building at Killingworth New Town, on the outskirts of Newcastle, establishing the practice's reputation for innovative and highly individual modern buildings, and winning the RIBA Award in 1966. The client's requirements for maximum flexibility led to a design which simplified the main accommodation and internal arrangements of the building, allowing them to be completely flexible to changing business requirements.

Opposite: Gordon Ryder and Peter Yates, c.1971

The building demonstrated the controlled quality of the work of Ryder and Yates, subtly related to levels, textures and movement. The use of colour, of gently moving water, of the reflection in glass, and of imagery was executed with masterly assurance and deceptive simplicity. However, the building design was criticised by Walter Gropius, in a letter in the *Architectural Review*, for what he saw as an inappropriate use of Minoan imagery in the form of the roof light to the restaurant block (in much the same way that Lubetkin had been taken to task for his use of caryatids in Highpoint II).

A second commission at Killingworth, for British Gas, led to the design of the Engineering Research Station, winner of the Financial Times Industrial Architecture Award for 1968 and an RIBA Award in 1969. This building demonstrated their uniqueness, inventiveness and innovation in a way that challenged traditional architecture and engineering ideas. The Engineering Research Station, a building that owed as much to the doctrines of Le Corbusier's villas as to the industrial designs of Walter Gropius, became arguably their best-known building. Its uncompromising design concept led to the building being described by the *Architects' Journal* as 'pure architecture'.

The Engineering Research Station consisted of two distinct sections, a fixed element which included entrance, library, administration and car park, and a flexible section for offices, laboratories and workshops – all encased in a regular box of painted concrete panels and ribbon windows, lending a formality to the exterior that belied the indeterminate nature of the interior. The permanent element, with its symbolic bridge and pylon, proclaimed itself structurally and formally, by a group of six roof towers.

Gordon Ryder's approach to architecture was to redefine building design so that it became non-representational, nothing taken for granted. All the accepted vocabulary was re-examined, rejected or refined until it became abstract. Consequently, his buildings did not conform to any visual formula but were designed from the same philosophical outlook of reducing the design to its simplest plan and form. Items normally hidden were expressed as a visual feature, an extension of the functionalist ideal.

That philosophy was extended throughout the next two decades not only in his own house, but also in major buildings for the Salvation Army, Tyne Tees Television, MEA House and Vickers Armaments, buildings that have redefined and reshaped the architectural landscape of Newcastle.

Over a period of 30 years, Gordon Ryder never lost sight of his commitment to modernism, the second generation of the Modern Movement, and pursued it with vigour even after most of his contemporaries had rejected it. It has often been said that architecture is a social art and as such reflects society. The architects of the 1960s, like their predecessors, were convinced that they alone knew what society wanted and in those idealist days, they alone could provided it.

Ryder and Yates, even in their chosen North Eastern isolation, endorsed those views and consistently put them into practice with their buildings. The importance of this period in the later development of modern architecture is now becoming apparent. A recent recommendation of post-war listing included a number of designs by Ryder and Yates, a timely reminder of the major contribution that the practice has made to the development of modern architecture in the North East of England.

Privately, Gordon was first and foremost a family man. He and his wife Mary were accomplished sailors, spending many wonderful holidays sailing around the Mediterranean with their four children. In retirement, Gordon was able to spend more time with Mary, their children, grandchildren and great grandchildren, and enjoying his other great passions of model making and music.

Gordon was a wonderful host and teller of anecdotal stories, which he constantly embellished, much to the delight of his listeners. Charmingly flirtatious, highly intelligent with a marvellous sense of humour, Gordon did not suffer fools gladly, but to his many friends and acquaintances he offered true friendship and generosity. He continued to live life to the full, long after his retirement, never losing his passionate interest in architecture or the firm, which has continued much in the spirit upon which it was founded. Gordon Ryder was much loved and will be sadly missed.

Rutter Carroll
RIBA Newsletter, January 2001

Yates on View

(This article is an extended version of a piece that appeared in *The Observer*, Sunday, 22 September 1985.)

Architecture

In an exhibition at the RIBA (September 1985), you see the artist at work through a collection of paintings and prints by the late Peter Yates, and how very refreshing this experience is. Being a modest man who was committed to his art, whether this was expressed through buildings or paintings, little was really known about Yates when he died in 1982, aged 62. Yet the biographical notes in the catalogue showed that he had achieved an immense amount in his comparatively short life; he had been drawing from his childhood onwards, had worked as a commercial artist in Fleet Street after he left school, was making paintings of the incendiary attacks on London from St Paul's Cathedral in 1941 (when a fireman), and continued to do so when he was in the invasion of France where he came across Le Corbusier, Gertrude Stein, Steinberg and others. But by this time he had already studied architecture and engineering.

And after this period, in 1945, he was working for Ove Arup on a competition entry for the new Crystal Palace in the form of a dramatic glass and concrete pyramid that was designed in collaboration with Le Corbusier (a classical design was the winner, but never built); and, three years later, he was assisting Berthold Lubetkin on the master plan for Peterlee New Town. In 1950, however, he was back in Paris running a commercial art firm and designing exhibitions all over Europe. And so, by the time he joined Gordon Ryder in Newcastle in 1953 to practise architecture, Peter Yates was a highly experienced designer who used every form of visual expression to impart his ideas; and from this it can be seen that the present collection of his paintings and prints would have been regarded by him as an extremely significant contribution to his work as an artist.

Painting, one feels, was for him a somewhat private area of his remarkable imagination, a means of commenting on places visited in his vast travels across England and Europe, or of fixing some very special image that had to be remembered for some future project. For what emerges from this exhibition is an astonishingly clear eye for colour, form and atmosphere; every idea is perfectly observed and executed; a message about a subject is exactly communicated, without blemish. It is, of course, always difficult to say which will have been responsible for what, in their remarkable stream of buildings in Newcastle – whether it was Ryder or Yates – because the imagination in architecture is often a mysterious product of an intricate rapport between minds. All the same, one identifies in them a brilliant graphic sense that one finds here, in these pictures.

Stephen Gardiner 1985

Bibliography

Periodicals and journals

Architects' Journal, 21 May 1969, 'Northern Lights', Architectural exhibition at Newcastle featuring works by Ryder and Yates

Northern Architect, G. Ryder, 'Architect/engineer relationship'

Architects' Journal, 20 January 1971, pp154–8, 'Ryder and Yates'

Northern Echo, 18 November 1971, 'Prizes keep coming for partners in success'. Profile of Ryder and Yates partnership

Architect, September 1972, 'Mirror Walling'

Building Design Magazine, 12 September 1975, 'Practice Makes Perfect'

Northern Architect, October 1975, Peter Yates, 'Ideas'

Architects' Journal, 12 November 1975, 'Ryder and Yates: Architects' Approach to Architecture'

Observer Magazine, 7 November 1976, 'Britain's Architects', featuring Gordon Ryder

RIBA Journal, January 1976, 'Ryder and Yates and Partners: Approach to Architecture' pp18–28

Northern Architect, January 1976, Peter Yates, 'Ideas'

Architects' Journal, January 1981, 'Architects' Architecture'

The Journal, 30 January 1997, 'Shining reward for glass of genius', listing of ERS

The Journal, October 1993, 'Beautiful or Gas-tly', series of articles on the proposed listing of Norgas House

Perspectives, January 1995, pp36–7, Alan Powers, 'Welcoming the new pretenders', potential listing of Liddell House

Daily Telegraph, 15 March 1995, 'Dorrell seeks views of modern buildings', potential listing of both Norgas House and Ryder and Yates' offices

The Journal, 15 March 1995, 'Sixties office blocks are building up to make the grade', potential listing of both Norgas House and Ryder and Yates's offices

Financial Times, 20 March 1995, 'A chance to choose', potential listing of both Norgas House and Ryder and Yates's offices

The Journal, 19 April 1997, 'Officials get keys to 2.1 m site', North Tyneside Council buys the former Engineering Research Station

Architect, July 1973, pp52–4, Profile of a practice 7, Ryder & Yates and Partners'

Books

John Allan, *Berthold Lubetkin*, RIBA Publications Ltd, London, 1992
Bruce Allsop, *Modern Architecture of Northern England*, Oriel Press, Newcastle, 1969
P. Coe and M. Reading, *Lubetkin and Tecton*, Arts Council, London, 1981
Garry Philipson, *Aycliffe and Peterlee New Towns 1946–1988*, Publications for
    Companies, Cambridge, 1988

Reports

Peterlee: Analysis of Planning Problems, 'Report of the Architect Planner',
edited by Gordon Ryder, 16 January 1950
SDA Selective Design Allocation Thinking about Building, Reports 1–4
edited by Ted Nicklin

Articles on Ryder and Yates

Docomomo UK Newsletter, autumn 1995, Rutter Carroll, 'Ryder and Yates: Continuing
    the Lubetkin Legacy'
20th Century Society Newsletter, 2004, pp6–7, Rutter Carroll, 'Ryder and Yates'
The Journal, 19 November 2005, p16, Tony Henderson, 'Ryder and Yates's Social
    Housing'
Journal of Architecture, autumn 2001, pp225–48, Peter Fawcett, 'Learning from le
    Corbusier and Lubetkin: the work of Ryder and Yates'

Obituaries

Guardian, 17 March 1994, 'Ted Nicklin, 1925–1994'
RIBA Newsletter, March 1994, Peter Buchan, 'Ted Nicklin, 1925–94'
The Journal, January 2000, Rutter Carroll, 'Gordon Ryder OBE, 1919–2000'
RIBA North Newsletter, January 2001, Rutter Carroll, 'Gordon Ryder OBE, 1919–2000'
20th Century Newsletter, May 2001, Obituary on Gordon Ryder by Rutter Carroll

Index

Note: Italic page numbers refer to illustrations

Picture Credits

The original source of most of the photographs was the Ryder and Yates archive, within the Ryder office. The author and publisher have made every effort to contact copyright holders and will be happy to correct, in subsequent editions, any errors or omissions that are brought to their attention.

We are indebted to the family of Peter Yates for permission to use copies of his paintings in this publication.

Our thanks to the Ryder office for redrawing the original architect's drawings specifically for inclusion in this publication.

© FLC / ADAGP, Paris and DACS, London 2009 – p4

© FLC / ADAGP, Paris and DACS, London 2009 – pxvi

© Richard Bryant / arcaid.co.uk – pp101, 102, 104, 113, 131

Architectural Press Archive / © RIBA Library Photographs Collection – back cover and pp14, 20 (top), 29, 134

Estate of Gordon Ryder – pp2, 36 (top)

Estate of Peter Yates – ppxvi, 2, 4, 5, 6, 8, 11, 13, 38, 50, 58, 62, 88, 114 (bottom), 120, 122, 124, 132

Henk Snoek / © RIBA Library Photographs Collection – front cover and pp25, 31, 41 (left), 43, 44 (both), 73, 75, 76, 78, 79, 81, 93, 94, 114 (top), 118, 129

James Riddell – pp40, 60

London News Agency Photos Ltd – pp53, 54

P.I.C. Photos Ltd. – p56

Philipson Studios – pp41 (right), 47, 66, 68, 90 (top), 91, 98 (bottom), 108 (bottom), 109, 110 (bottom), 112

Photo-Mayo Ltd. – ppii, 64, 71, 82, 83, 84, 85, 95, 97

Ryder and Yates Archive – ppvi, 10, 12, 17, 18, 19, 20 (bottom), 22 (both), 23, 24, 32, 33, 34, 36 (bottom) 38, 52, 61 (both), 65, 69, 70, 74, 77, 80, 82, 90 (bottom), 92 (both), 96, 98 (top), 99, 103, 108 (top), 110 (top), 111, 117, 127

Tothill Press Ltd. (Ryder and Yates Archive) – pp27, 125